MW00748087

Gender, Participation and Silence in the Language Classroom

Gender, Participation and Silence in the Language Classroom

Sh-shushing the Girls

Allyson Julé

First published 2004 by
PALGRAVE MACMILLAN
Houndmills, Basingstoke, Hampshire RG21 6XS and
175 Fifth Avenue, New York, N. Y. 10010
Companies and representatives throughout the world

PALGRAVE MACMILLAN is the global academic imprint of the Palgrave Macmillan division of St. Martin's Press, LLC and of Palgrave Macmillan Ltd. Macmillan® is a registered trademark in the United States, United Kingdom and other countries. Palgrave is a registered trademark in the European Union and other countries.

ISBN 1–4039–1583–0

This book is printed on paper suitable for recycling and made from fully managed and sustained forest sources.

A catalogue record for this book is available from the British Library.

Library of Congress Cataloging-in-Publication Data
Julé, Allyson, 1965–
        Gender, participation, and silence in the language classroom : sh-shushing the girls / Allyson Julé.
            p. cm.
        Includes bibliographical references and index.
        ISBN 1–4039–1583–0 (cloth)
            1. Language and languages—Study and teaching. 2. Gender identity in education. 3. Language and languages—Sex differences. 4. Minorities--Education. 5. Women—Language. I. Title.

P53.J85 2003
418'.0071—dc22
                                                                    2003061601

10   9   8   7   6   5   4   3   2   1
13   12   11   10   09   08   07   06   05   04

Printed and bound in Great Britain by
Antony Rowe Ltd, Chippenham and Eastbourne

To Marvin,
for time lost ...

Contents

Acknowledgements

I welcome this opportunity to express my gratitude to the many people who helped me through the relatively lonely process of writing this book. At the University of Surrey - Roehampton, London, UK, Professor Pat Mahony and Professor Jen Coates, and at the Institute of Education, London, Professor Graham Welch, three dedicated scholars I was fortunate to have guiding and supporting my doctoral work. I am grateful to them for their wisdom and enthusiasm. I am also so very thankful to Dr Kelleen Toohey at Simon Fraser University, Canada, for her early belief in me and this project, and to RIIM for its initial funding.

I am deeply indebted to two colleagues who became my friends: first, to Cheryl Wall at Trinity Western University, Canada, for her skill and tenacious patience with the transcriptions and keyboarding needs; and second, to Dr Judith Baxter at the University of Reading, UK, for her interest, her intelligence, and her graciousness in reading various drafts of the book. I am grateful.

To Jill Lake and Paula Kennedy at Palgrave Macmillan for their interest in this book and their support regarding its completion. I also wish to thank my sister, Nikki Niles, for her clever cover design. Thank you! I am also very grateful to the students and staff at the University of Glamorgan, Wales, with whom I discussed many of the ideas developed in the book. I am also eternally grateful for the children and staff at the Punjabi school in Canada, who welcomed me warmly into their classrooms, their temples, their homes, and their lives. 'Shu-kri-ya!'

And, as ever and forever, I am so very grateful for the staggering support of Dr Marvin Lemke (Marv) and of our children, Clark and Jane. Their steady patience with me and their divine devotion to my ventures always make all the difference. To Clark and Jane, this is especially for you and your generation: Speak what you feel.

'Speak what we feel,
not what we ought to say...'
(in *King Lear,* V. iii. 324)

Introduction:
Silence and Second Language Learning

This book sets out to examine how it is that silence in language classrooms may have something to do with the construction of gender roles in the classroom itself and in particular pedagogical methods. In much language and gender research, girls have been routinely shown as quiet classroom participants. However, the language classroom appears to have been relatively ignored in such studies. Hence, this book. The language learning classroom is a context worth exploring for evidence of speech and silence and possible explanations as to why or how the classroom habits create certain consistent behaviors. The girls in the classroom I visited and studied were very quiet little girls at certain times. In particular, they said very little to contribute to their whole-class lessons during the literacy hour each morning. Why was this? Did they just so happen to be quiet in temperament? Were they primed to be quiet by their particular culture? Could the implication within this latter question be an erroneous and even lazy yet common assumption within the field of language acquisition (that 'they can be like that')? Might the language learning girls I observed have been constructed by the habits and practices of their particular classroom into such silent participation? If not (if they are quiet of their own accord), then the arguments can return to anthropology or sociology or psychology for discussion of the cultural values and behavior of particular groups. But if their behavior can be seen to be promoted by the classroom dynamics, and if in fact the teaching methods may be even partly implicated in the girls' lack of verbal participation,

1

then the field of second/foreign language teaching is compelled to explore how it could be so in its search for effective language teaching practice.

It is for this reason that I have set out to describe the 'sh-shushing' of a group of ethnic-minority girls, as I feel the particular classroom under investigation offers insights that could well advance a deeper understanding of gender in language education.

In Part I of this book entitled 'Intersubjectivity, Gender, and Language Classrooms,' I set out Lacan's (1968) view of belonging, what he called 'intersubjectivity,' and apply it to a language classroom. Gender as a variable has long been argued to impose marginality on females. Ethnicity too. But these two factors together may be uniquely seen in language classroom students. They are significant factors independent of each other, but together they offer a further example of the often perceived illegitimacy of female participants in mixed group settings, possibly experienced by other girls in other language classrooms today.

It is, therefore, so very important for the field of second/foreign language acquisition to attempt to understand the role gender may play in producing or prompting certain participation patterns among some female students. It is the relative exclusion of gender from language-learning teacher education and research (TESL) that has led me to explore a particular application of Lacan's theory of intersubjectivity alongside feminist educational thought within language education.

Perhaps ideas, like those expressed by Faludi (1993) in her analysis of popular and political cultures as in a 'backlash' against feminism, provide some explanation as to the battle fatigue expressed in many circles – sentiments such as 'Not this again!' And yet I feel the time is ripe for more, perhaps different, discussions concerning gender in language education because it has been largely ignored in such classrooms while debates have flourished elsewhere. While feminists, including feminist linguists and feminist pedagogues, continue to revise and revisit feminist theory (as seems necessary in each generation), the need to take into account language classrooms seems to be a relatively fresh one (Sunderland, 1994, 1995, 1998; Vandrick, 1999a, 1999b; Norton, 2000). When we examine ethnicity, we seem to ignore gender; or we explore gender but then separate it from the influence of ethnicity (discussed in Hull et al., 1982, *All the Blacks are Men, All the Women are White*). That the two variables may be so intertwined, revealing each other in certain ways and both able to be constructed inside classrooms, is an intuitive truth that needs to be articulated in as many ways as possible and, therefore, needs to be more seriously debated among language educators.

Part II, 'A Case Study of One Room, One Voice,' seeks to do this exact thing: to examine the role of gender alongside ethnicity in a language classroom. The particular peculiarities of one classroom may distract or shrink away from larger, more generalizable studies (such as AAUWEF, 1992, though this exhaustive study fails to specifically implicate language classrooms). Every classroom anywhere in the world has its local details, each apt to call out, 'It's different here!' However, the point of qualitative work is precisely to say, 'This is one case,' and not attempt to offer statistics or percentages as conclusions to apply to other situations. There are never simple conclusions to the ever-complex context of schooling, and certainly the role gender plays in the midst of it is one that will continue to be ever-new because the people and places are ever-changing. There are no conclusions to the matter here. There has never been, nor will there ever be, a final conclusion to the matter of gender and education, which is exactly why we seek further understanding about it. A little more helps a little more.

It is also a tradition among writing concerned with gender, particularly feminist writing, to present individual, intimate accounts, such as a single case (Lather, 1991; Acker, 1994). Also, most feminist work includes 'the self' as central to the story being told. To some extent, I follow this lead. This case study of one classroom involves me too. (I am most often referred to as 'Ally' in the classroom conversations.) In this way, the case study uses the usual ethnographic methods, particularly participant-observation, as its main form of data collection. The example of one classroom allows for a specific and intimate look, a glimpse in passing, at the language used and at the linguistic space used and the verbal participation among certain students at a particular time in a particular place. That the girls in this language classroom speak so rarely is explored with classroom practices and teaching methods emerging as chief concerns.

By Part III of the book, 'Sh-shushing Girls in Language Classrooms,' my humble concluding thoughts seem to settle on the early feminist view (as early as Wollstonecraft, 1791, *The Vindication of the Rights of Women*), that males are often the legitimate participants in mixed public groups and that most participants (both males and females) collude to allow males greater linguistic space. This is revealed and made evident in the amount of male-talk and the vibrancy of it in this classroom. Ultimately, the girls in this language classroom seem to serve a familiar role of audience to the richer dynamics between the teacher and the male students.

As a result, a continually compelling theme returns: to explore gender and to use this exploration to build new awareness of its remarkable, often frustrating, force in behavior. The role of 'voice' has a long tradition in feminist work: giving voice to intimate realities and perceptions and, ultimately perhaps, giving voice to the injustice or irrationality of gender roles (Gilligan, 1992; Acker, 1994). This combined with the apparently equally arbitrary element of ethnicity seems to serve certain groups as a compound fracture: a double whammy of de-centered power. ESL language students in white-western society have much to navigate through and, therefore, the language classrooms in which they live their educational experience need to be examined.

My role of participant-observer

As an educational ethnographer, I include a brief personal history here in the introduction of this book because, along with other current researchers, I consider it important for the reader to know, to some extent, where I have come from and what past linguistic and social positions I too have occupied.

As a young girl in the 1970s, I assumed a maternal and domestic role was one to be in my future, and I believe I felt certain ways and said certain things because of gender role expectations in place in my family and community. Perhaps my perceptions could be viewed as 'typical'. I believe I became a language teacher largely because this role seemed easily open to me as a woman. Throughout my early years as a classroom teacher, however, I became increasingly intrigued with the success of my male language students over the success of my female students in class discussions. Somehow I assumed that female students would be better participatory speakers, and yet I did not find this to be the case in my classrooms among my language-learning students. I certainly did not see girls speaking more than boys. Such personal discoveries and curiosities contributed to my early questions surrounding the role of gender in language education. My teaching experiences with the Canadian Punjabi Sikhs fueled my interest in this particular group.

But I am not Punjabi Sikh. Born white in Montreal, I grew up in a small Catholic community in a large predominantly English-Protestant city on the Canadian prairies, Edmonton. My French-Canadian father spoke both French and English; my Irish-Canadian mother spoke only English. As a result, we spoke only English at home; French was sometimes encouraged and spoken at occasional family events on my father's side. I saw and see myself as a Canadian—both French and Irish in heritage, functioning exclusively in English. My Catholic childhood home and my Catholic suburban schooling in particular were major moral and cultural influences on me and my sense of who I was. While in some ways being located as a member of a marginalized (ethnic/religious) group within an English-speaking, largely Protestant society, I grew up unaware of more ethnically marginalized groups. I saw most people through the lens of their religion (Protestant or Catholic), for this factor seemed most significant to my Catholic parents and the school and local community of which I was a part.

My impression now is that the immigrant experience known to many Canadians was one that I understood only from my French and Irish grandparents and the stories of their early experiences in Canada. However, I always felt 'Canadian' and far removed from a sense of foreignness. It was not until I was an adult and traveled to France and Ireland to visit distant relatives that I gave a great deal more thought to how I was French, Irish, Catholic, and Canadian and the extent to which such ethnicities influenced my sense of the world.

In addition to these personal details, I grew up at a particular historic time in Canada. I attended school after Trudeau's 1969 Official Languages Act, the Act which proclaimed Canada officially bilingual in English and French (Canada, 1970, 1971, 1988; Trudeau, 1984; Fleras and Elliot, 1992). As a result, I always studied French in school to meet graduation requirements. Mine was the first generation to be required to do so.

I grew up witnessing the frustration of many newer immigrant groups with official bilingualism, many who felt their contributions to Canada were ignored to appease Quebec (c.f. Trudeau, 1984; Fleras and Elliot, 1992; Ghosh, 1996). At my Catholic school, children of various ethnic groups populated the classrooms: Italian, Polish, Ukrainian, Filipino, Portuguese, Irish, and also French. (I do not recall any British descendants at the Catholic school, but there may have been one or two.) All these ethnic groups were together because of a shared Catholic faith. All of the students spoke English and experienced a level of embarrassment at school events when their parents did not. I believe cultural assimilation was the goal of the teachers, the parents, and certainly the students themselves—mastery of and use of English being the goal of all participants. I never heard my friends speak anything other than English at school, in spite of the different languages spoken in their homes. (This phenomenon is well articulated in Cummins, 1993, 1996.)

Unlike ESL/language students, I grew up always able to speak English, as did my parents. And I am white, while many language students in Canada are not white; such 'visibility' creates a different set of social realities for them that I did not encounter as a Catholic girl. Though the place at the margins, away from the English-Protestant norm, is perhaps similar, creating a similar 'otherness' from the Canadian mainstream, the visibility of the students I look at in this book connect with their ethnicity in a way much different from my connection with my ethnicity. This major distinction I admit, in spite of a connection I felt with the students. A shared position at the margins of English-Protestant Canadian society was perhaps largely in my own imagination and not in theirs.

Working definitions

A few working definitions are offered at the onset. The first concerns the use of the term 'ESL' (English as a Second Language). Though 'ELL' (English Language Learner) or 'EAL' (English as an Additional Language) or 'ELT' (English Language Teaching) are becoming preferred terms used to identify language students and language teaching in Britain, I continue to use the term 'ESL' (English as a Second Language) and/or 'TESL' (Teachers of/or Teaching of English as a Second Language) because they are more understood and recognized in the Canadian context where the study itself is based. The students in this study are identified as ESL students and not EFL (English as a Foreign Language) students because they are not studying English abroad, nor have plans to live anywhere other than Canada; they are Canadian citizens with a home language different from the English mainstream. A look at gender in ESL differs from gender explorations in EFL (such as well articulated by Sunderland, 1994, 1998) because of the strong particulars of the localized immigrant context.

The term 'Punjabi' is used to refer to the students' ethnicity rather than 'Indian'. In Canada, the term 'Punjabi' is used in the vernacular and as a way to distinguish this group from those of a Hindu-Indian heritage. In the British context, 'Asian' or even inaccurately 'Pakistani' or 'Bangladeshi' may be used to identify the ethnic heritage explored in this language classroom, but such terms would not be understood in the same way in Canada. For Canadians, the term 'Asian' refers to those who are Chinese or Japanese or those from other oriental groups and not those from India. In Canada, the term 'Indian' is more often the term still casually used to refer to the aboriginal tribes native to North America; 'East Indian' has also been used in the recent past to refer to those of South-Asian ancestry. The Punjabi Sikhs in Canada can be referred to as 'Indo-Canadians', though this term may also refer to immigrants from India of different language and religious populations. Hence, 'Punjabi' and/or 'Punjabi Sikh' will generally be used throughout the book. These differences in terms highlight some of the few differences between the British and Canadian language education communities. (See Edwards and Redfern, 1992, and Bannerji, 2000, for a fuller discussion of British and Canadian differences regarding multiculturalism and diversity and the Punjabi Sikh community in particular.)

Perhaps it goes without saying that the term 'gender' is used as distinct from the term 'sex'. Most people are born either biologically female (with XX chromosomes) or biologically male (with XY chromosomes). Certainly such biology determines aspects of anatomy and physiology (referred to as 'sex'), but such biology may also have a role in shaping behavioral and cognitive characteristics (referred to as 'gender'). But gender, unlike sex, is not a fixed category. A group of girls (or boys) may all demonstrate characteristics that may be understood by community members as generalizable to all girls (or all boys), but such characteristics or the meanings of these characteristics may differ from group to group and culture to culture (Nanda, 2000).

This book explores the construction of gendered behaviors by examining teaching approaches; therefore, 'gender' and not 'sex' is used to refer to this force in the human experience. That some students are girls may impact on language opportunities and participation in the language classroom. I acknowledge that the use of the terms 'boys' and 'girls' suggests an essentialist assumption about gender identities as fixed, an assumption I hope to argue against. However, I continue to use the terms in spite of the extensive debates surrounding the assumptions embedded in the terms (Crawford, 1995; Baxter, 1999). I do so mainly because they are terms most easily and clearly understood. And, in keeping with Lather's (1991) commitment to self-reflection in feminist research, I am explicit about such choices. In spite of my using the terms 'boys' and 'girls', I hold to a feminist post-structuralist view that we cannot assume gender categories and that it is possible to collapse notions of only two distinct genders for the sake of more complex, multiple identities (Baxter, 1999; Nanda, 2000). I also hold to the view that all participants are free agents and are active (though not necessarily aware) in creating their identities.

This book: ethnic-minority girls in language education

The past twenty-five years in particular have presented educators with a wealth of research on what happens to girls in schools. Arguably, some ESL girls have benefited from this research (Sunderland, 1994, 1995, 1998; Yepez, 1994). However, some researchers have argued that the female language-learning experience has been largely ignored (Cohran, 1996; Willett, 1996; Ehrlich, 1997; Vandrick, 1999a, 1999b). To respond to a perceived lack of language-learning research in pedagogy, this book uses Lacan's intersubjective theoretical frame to focus on the spoken experiences of a language classroom comprised of Punjabi Sikh Canadian children and with their non-Punjabi Canadian teacher with a particular focus on the silent participation of the girls.

This book is also in keeping with the fascination with gender across many academic disciplines, much of it still suggesting that girls or women do not receive equal attention from society nor adequate opportunities to speak in various public forums (Gilligan, 1992; Orenstein, 1994; Sadker and Sadker, 1994; Aries, 1997; Gambell and Hunter, 2000). This curiosity has influenced classroom research and teacher training programs. But Willett (1996) has asked, 'Why has the TESOL profession taken so long to examine gender? Whose stories are being told in our research?' (p. 344). Vandrick (1999b) added to this saying, 'Now we need to find out which research results apply to ESL students and classrooms' (p. 16). Now is the time.

Part I

Intersubjectivity, Language Classrooms, and Gender

1

Intersubjectivity in Language Classrooms

The word 'intersubjectivity' simply means a collection of individual subjectivities or perceptions of reality. As a theory, intersubjectivity sees human subjectivity not as a private 'inner world', separate from an objective outer world, but as social relationships intersecting with individual 'inner worlds' or 'self-hoods' (Lacan, 1968). Relationships create participation; relationships create identity; therefore, participation creates identity. As such, relationships and one's participation within them are fundamental in the theory of intersubjectivity and the understanding of one's identity as embedded in a group. With this theoretical approach, classroom relationships are seen as critical in that they construct one's sense of self—relationships create the individual identity. The relationships which surround language students in their ESL classrooms can therefore partly construct participation through speech opportunities as well as through silence. Who is speaking and who is being silent (or silenced) are important questions because they reveal participation and, therefore, belonging.

Crossley (1996) attempted to define intersubjectivity and to understand why or how people 'feel' that they belong to a particular group. He ultimately settled on intersubjectivity as:

A situation in which space and time ... are shared, where each person speaks for themselves and where the intentions, thoughts and feelings of the one unfold before the other, calling forth responses from that other; ...

where people can be in their unique individuality for each other, where they see and are seen in the flesh and can correct misconceptions which may arise about themselves. (p. 82)

I believe intersubjectivity can be a helpful theory in understanding the role and the significance of a classroom community because of the role of the group in the construction of personal identity. Personal behavior (such as speech and silence) is seen as formed by relationships built through mutual and emotional recognition. In fact, Lacan believed that recognition was central to belonging because the relationships, embedded in any given community (such as family communities, ethnic communities, and classroom communities), are based on shared recognition of roles, behaviors, values. For Lacan, language was seen as the powerful intersubjective structure necessary for the shaping of identity and participation, because language practices could be understood and recognized by participants in a particular community. Shared cultural and language practices, then, could create community boundaries of both inclusion and exclusion and important points of reference because of features that are recognized and understood by present participants. With such a theory, language practices, such as a hybrid use of English or particularly gendered speech tendencies, are significant indicators of participation and belonging and ultimately create the shared inner worlds of community participants.

The mirror stage

One particularly important facet in the concept of recognition within a group is what Lacan called the 'mirror stage'. Lacan's mirror stage is a metaphor based on a developmental stage in infancy where it is believed that an infant recognizes herself in a mirror only after, it is assumed, she has recognized another in the mirror first (such as her mother). The key process here that is fundamental to learning is this recognition of another first before being able to locate oneself in the surrounding environment. From this, Lacan understood that personal identity is deeply embedded in the people who are present with us—those who are within the frame and recognizable to us as present participants. With a recognition of others, one feels connection. From such a connection, there is a sense of participation and belonging that supports identity formation and constructs language development for use within that community.

Wilden (1981) particularly illuminated how intersubjectivity may impact on the notion of 'self' as a physical presence:

> The key point here is the notion of totality. The narcissistic component of the child (or man) who sees himself in the other, without realizing that what he contemplates as his self *is* the other, is quite different from that which is commonly thought to mean an autoerotic relationship between the subject and his own body (or parts of it). As others had said before Lacan, it is the notion of the *body image* which is involved rather than the notion of the body itself. (p. 173)

This mirrored-self, if different or deficient in a body-image way from the others in the frame, is problematic. An absence of recognition of physical traits may be particularly critical in understanding ethnic-minority language children. In English mainstream classrooms, minority children of visible groups may find themselves objectified in the gaze of the white, mainstream others, unrecognisable within a larger Western culture—beyond the mirrored frame. The characteristics needed for recognition by those around each of us can potentially enhance or limit recognition and, as a result, construct an 'outside'. Crossley (1996) explained that the self as participant based on the recognition of others has much to do with the perceived superiority or legitimacy of the other, viewed both by individuals involved and by the collective society. He wrote, 'The struggle to be recognized is [also] a struggle to be distinctive and valued within a group' (p. 66). It is the construction of one's identity as based on the perception of others that intersubjectivity attempts to both describe and explain.

Crossley's discussion of the role of language in this process is helpful in understanding a classroom community and the role it plays in the experiences of any given individual. Such an understanding of groups may illuminate the processes within language classrooms. The community of the classroom may recognize a shared ethnic heritage and be able to negotiate meaning through participation in dialogue—or it may not.

Language as a dimension of intersubjectivity: inclusion and exclusion

Language practices and strategies can embrace gender recognition and gender construction as well as ethnicity. As part of intersubjectivity, speech is 'necessarily meaningful' in that certain discursive patterns derive from and are created by surrounding relationships (Crossley, 1996, p. 8). Because an awareness of self is believed to involve an awareness of others, the particular role of speech and certain 'speech acts' as community patterns can indicate who belongs and to whom in classroom grouping. Buber (1958) wrote, 'Language is not transcendental in this view. It belongs to the life of a community, as an institution, and it is activated in praxis as the structuring principle of that praxis' (p. 14).

In light of these notions of belonging, ESL students can be understood as partly dependent on a shared ethnic context, with those whom there is some basic congruence. With a view of intersubjectivity, an individual is constructed by the community of participants who recognize and reinforce roles through particular language patterns (a view also used in the classroom research of Lave and Wenger, 1991, as well as many others).

And yet, Crossley (1996), following Merleau-Ponty (1962), explored the self as temporarily experiencing dislocation over an objectified or unrecognized form of the self or others and the loss of a determinance of one's own actions. This occurs if the 'others' in a community are not recognized and no reference point is found to produce a sense of belonging. If a community is so central in defining and describing an individual, then a dependence on others for recognition may be a particularly anxious experience if dominant 'others' have inadequate understanding or only a partly shared cultural context—if, in fact, there is any cultural or linguistic recognition at all. To be observed and defined by a group of others can be alienating and risky. Crossley thought that visible minorities, those defined as 'other' within a Western culture in this case, may be examples of intersubjective frustration because they have to see themselves as always 'different' from a normative reference point and, as a result, consistently unrecognized and, therefore, excluded.

Merleau-Ponty (1962) explored this social nature of language and linguistic meaning. He saw thinking itself as a shared social activity and, therefore, always intersubjective in character. He believed that thought itself was intersubjective (not just the language code) and that, as a result, there are no private mental thoughts. From this view, the language of a group carries the meaning of thoughts and perceptions and the creation of thoughts and perceptions.

Taylor (1994) more recently also explored 'recognition' in the lives of minority or visible participants in Western contexts. He said:

> What has come about with the modern age is not the need for recognition but the conditions in which the attempt to be recognized can fail. That is why the need is now acknowledged for the first time. In premodern times, people didn't speak of 'identity' and 'recognition'—not because people didn't have (what we call) identities, or because these didn't depend on recognition, but rather because these were then too unproblematic to be thematized as such. (p. 35)

Identity in this book is understood from a constructionist perspective and not a psychological one per se. Regardless of where identity rests (in an individual or in a collective), the notion of intersubjectivity as a collection or mixing of subjectivities serves as a compelling response to long-held assimilationist views in language education. ESL students are a part of a larger Canadian, English-speaking society that may require them to be members of particular communities and similar enough to 'mirror back' a recognizable vision of themselves as members. If this does not occur, these students can be excluded from belonging to a mainstream 'Canadian' classroom community. Paradoxically, the segregation of one-culture schools may provide a way for ESL students to build personal identities in harmony with their given heritage, a place where they recognize others and are recognized by them. From this place of participation and belonging, they may be able to emerge with a sense of themselves as both a part of something Punjabi (in the case study explored in Part II of this book) as well as a part of a mainstream multicultural Canadian society.   This is the hope of culturally specific schooling and provides justification, to some extent, as to why such schools exist in Canada and elsewhere. That is, minority students need to 'belong' first to each other before enlarging the frame of reference to include a larger Canadian identity.

Factors other than ethnicity can affect communication or the appropriation of a shared language code, such as age, social class, family history, nationality, education, and conversational styles, even within groups that are largely homogeneous.   Nevertheless, Kramsch (1993) also believed that the more similarities that exist in a classroom, the greater the sense of connection. The theory of intersubjectivity would support her view. The greater the sense of connection and shared understandings, the greater the context for possible discourse. Kramsch saw the exploration of language acquisition as a journey to discover the very social and cultural nature of language learning and not a search for good or bad classrooms. Her belief that language is community-based supports the claim that language is primarily and intimately contextual, living within any group.

In a search for explanations as to how language is so contextual, Rampton's (1995) thorough and exhaustive look at Punjabi and Afro-Caribbean adolescents in the United Kingdom explored how languages are mixed to allow for particular communication and belonging between language groups and within communities. He saw code-crossing as a process of intersecting ethnic difference with a highly complex set of situational contingencies, such as the stage and state of talk, the activity type, the institutional setting, and the relationship between interlocutors. Although there are no grounds for suggesting that the Punjabi adolescents in his study were exceptional in their interactional competence, code-crossing entailed some very skillful language negotiation around the meaning of ethnicity and belonging in the particular community. Hall's (1996) ideas also support Rampton's in suggesting that ethnic identities are so significant and central as social constructions that educators need to understand better the institutional sites where children negotiate their participation. Emerging from both Hall (1996) and Rampton (1995), language is contextual and the specific language strategies occurring within specific communities are infinitely unique and yet ultimately formational in creating participation and thereby identity (or identity and thereby participation). As such, classrooms serve a vital role.

Intersubjectivity: a philosophy for language classrooms

The theory of intersubjectivity is concerned with the manner in which the human consciousness or subjectivity is constructed through communities. Observation and recognition of and by another are central in understanding an individual's role. These particular perceptions and imaginings then are dependent on shared language and its frequent cultural referents; so language is therefore foundational in understanding intersubjectivity. By entering into participation by way of discourse, individual subjectivities transcend their own personal margins and become components of larger, intersubjective, whole communities (such as classrooms). Speech and language create the meanings bestowed on a group by the various individuals. It follows from this that there can be little self-knowledge without an awareness or recognition of the others in the group.

If self-hood emerges from intersubjectivity, a connection with others, intersubjectivity necessarily involves communication with 'the other'. This communication is conditional on recognition or influenced by the lack of it. In other words, relationships and language in ESL/language classrooms depend on recognition of similarities and/or differences with those in the room.

We perform many tasks by speaking; for example, we declare, ask, prohibit, request, command. It stands to reason that the effectiveness of participation through speech and through silence will be partly dependent on the relationships which surround the language users, requiring a shared agreement of meaning. If speech situations are embedded in social conditions which can determine who is able to speak and what is possible to say, then there is power woven into intersubjectivity. Classroom communities are not benign. Other critical theorists, like Habermas (1987) and Bourdieu (1992, 2001), also see language as socially located and socially constructed but also implemented in the creation of power for some and the oppression of others to support the powerful. Some speak and some do not. That the act of speaking is powerful may be subject to opinion, but I believe it is possible that in a language classroom the speakers may be the more powerful participants (more powerful than the listeners). The particular theory of intersubjectivity, as defined explicitly by Buber (1958), Merleau-Ponty (1962), and Lacan (1968), points to the collective relationships that make specific impact on self-hood and sees spoken language itself as the critical intersubjective tool. Speaking is central to self-hood.

The theory connects well with an understanding of ethnicity as well as the relationship of language and gender. Ethnicity and gender are both particular and powerful variables which impact on power, inclusion, exclusion, legitimacy, silence. Language classroom groups are unique combinations of complex subjectivities that connect and intersect in particular ways and ultimately through speech. If a large part of belonging to a group rests on shared recognition, such recognition could include ethnic or gender tendencies of behavior. I believe that the theory of intersubjectivity helps to explain the language classroom community because it helps to explain the meaning of speech acts and of silence.

2
Gender in Language Education

This chapter reviews the relevant research concerning gender and education, as well as the connection between gender and language use, with spoken language viewed as a key indicator of language classroom participation.

The specific structures surrounding classrooms are of particular interest in the larger gender and language debate (the largest study being AAUWEF, 1992). Many researchers have offered various pieces to the puzzle. For example, Oxford's (1994) work on gender differences in language classrooms focused on the particular learning styles noted in females and the particular language learning strategies often employed by females within language classrooms. After much discussion of the differences, such as subjectivity or objectivity, field dependence or independence, reflection or sensory preference among female second language learners, she concluded by suggesting that more research is necessary 'to understand better the relationships involved' (p. 147). She said:

> Anatomy is not destiny, as Freud suggested, but a learner's sex—or, more likely, gender—can have profound effects on the ways that learners approach language learning, ways which may in turn affect proficiency. More research is clearly needed to untie the Gordian knot of style and strategy differences between the sexes and to understand better the relationships involved. (p. 146-147)

I agree: much more research into language classrooms is needed to make larger claims, particularly to see if gender research in non-language learning classrooms apply directly to the language classroom with the added variable of ethnicity.

One of the themes running through the related work of Walkerdine (1990) is that all classrooms are sites of struggle—and often passive and silent struggles on the part of the many girls regardless of ethnicity. Struggles to participate may exist because of the particular power relations within the classroom, power which may be revealed in speech and silence. For example, the classrooms in Walkerdine's (1990) research revealed offensive and, at times, aggressive discourse on the part of male students to their female teachers and female classmates. Other studies, too, have found maleness as a major indicator of power and legitimacy as demonstrated through speech practices. Research that has focused on primary classrooms (nursery schools, reception classes, kindergarten) has explored discourse in the very early years (particularly Myers, 2000). Short and Carrington's (1989) research of young children's attitudes suggested the possibility that gender roles are prescribed early in life and are believed by the child to be relatively stable; that is, the child views his or her gender as a fixed element by the age of five. When the children in their study were asked explicitly about gender roles, they responded with traditional gender stereotyping comments; a significant number of children spoke of the traditional gender roles as 'natural'.

However, some roles or habits seem to suggest 'more power' is seen as male and 'less power' is seen as female. A lack of self-esteem among many girls may be the main point of concern when considering gender in the classroom because girls tend to describe themselves as fundamentally different from the way their boy classmates describe themselves. The evidence seems to be clear that girls, in general, offer comments to suggest that they are 'less', and reveal themselves as more self-demeaning and modest than boys in similar situations (Szirom, 1988). Such studies, then, seem to suggest both boys and girls participate in creating power differences.

Of particular concern to me in the understanding of speech and silence in language education is what Mahony (1985) first termed 'linguistic space'. Mahony found that it was 'normal' for a teacher to ignore girls for long periods of time, for boys to call out, and for boys to dominate classroom talk in addition to dominating the actual physical space. The evidence of gendered language tendencies in classrooms may derive from both the particular features of the language used (particular patterns) as well as the amount or proportion of talk-time in teacher-led lessons (that is, both the quality of language as well as the quantity).

Gender may well be revealed in language use, yet Bailey (1993) believed that 'few studies explore the way in which the language that is presented to children within the classroom context contributes to their developing gender awareness' (p. 8). She sees gender as constructed through language and that teachers pass on a social order through their own use of speech (i.e. patterns and proportions of talk-time).

Other earlier observational studies have examined what children do in classrooms when selecting certain toys or books. Such studies have also looked at which stories teachers read to children and how gender is presented in the stories and in the school culture itself by special events and the language used. The earlier interactional analysis work of Flanders (1970) also found teacher-dominated approaches in most classrooms, limiting student contributions in general and perhaps female contributions in particular. But these fascinating findings have not been specifically brought to bear on the language classroom or to language teacher training (Szirom, 1988; Burn, 1989).

According to Corson (1993), many studies have confirmed that teachers may be unaware of the fact that they over-talk. They also seem unaware that they treat boys so differently from girls and even disbelieve the evidence when confronted with it. Indeed, it may be common for teachers to defend their actual practices with the sincere disclaimer that they 'treat them all the same' (p. 144), as recorded in Corson's work.

Because classrooms are filled with language, language classrooms in particular, students are engaged with language for most of the day. If there are marked and consistent patterns in the ways girls participate in their classrooms, what are these tendencies and what are the implications? Spender and Sarah (1980) believed that girls were the ones who were ' 'learning how to lose' at the game of education undemanding of teacher time, passive, background observers to boys' active learning, ...and to strive for success within traditional, domestic, nurturing careers' (p. 27). And, regardless of test scores or academic achievement (recently in favour of girls worldwide), the girls' 'success' in education and throughout life remains a complex and contradictory issue. Higher test scores on the part of girls do not correlate with high academic achievement or high success-indication later in life (Davies, 1999).

Boys' underachievement

Recent research seems to suggest that it is the boys who are underachieving, 'learning how to lose,' in part due to a growing male culture which insists on a lack of interest in academic pursuits ('lad culture,' as it is commonly referred to in Britain) (Altani, 1995; Yates, 1997; Connell, 1996; Epstein et al, 1998; Davies, 1999; Mac an Ghaill, 2000). This possibility has led to what Davies (1999) refers to as a false 'moral panic' in society and a grappling for more classroom support for boys rather than for girls, to create 'better men'. This issue is an explosive one in Britain and elsewhere, including Canada, with boys' underachievement as a growing focus of much recent feminist discussions (Baxter, 1999, 2002; Mac an Ghaill, 2000).

However, such discussions seem to be settling on this underachievement of boys as unlikely to benefit girls in the long run because 'discursive practices continue to constitute girls' school successes in limited and derogatory ways' (Baxter, 1999, p. 94). Baxter believes that even if girls 'win' they still 'lose', 'winning' at tests but 'losing' at life. But regardless of which gender may be seen as 'losing out' in education (or maybe because of the confusion), gender remains a compelling variable to examine what influences academic experience. A consensus is far from imminent, and the feminist concerns (perhaps seen as part of a 1970s and 1980s agenda) are far from resolved with a current preoccupation with boys' underachievement (Mahony, 1998). Either way, gender matters.

Teacher talk

It has also long been argued that teacher attitudes toward gender within education have historical, structural, and ideological roots and that systematic attitudes toward gender are revealed in 'teacher talk' (Thornborrow, 2002). Such studies indicate gender discrimination in classrooms exists largely at a covert level (Lobban, 1978; Clarricoates, 1978, Delamont, 1980; Adelman, 1981; French and French, 1984, in Thompson, 1989). Thompson (1989) believed the coversion is because teachers seem to 'know what teaching is' not from teacher training programs (no matter how enlightened) but from their own previous classroom experiences as students; they thus largely perpetuate accepted attitudes from their past (p. 69). The majority of primary teachers in particular do not regard gender as a matter that is all that relevant to them.

Rather, primary teachers feel that they treat all children the same—as 'individuals'.

But Thornborrow's (2002) recent research highlights the ways that teachers control classroom participation through their teacher talk (reinforcing Flanders, 1970). She sees teacher talk as creating and maintaining asymmetrical power relationships. Teacher-led classroom talk as a pedagogical approach is often organized around initiation/response/follow-up exchanges, in which the teacher controls the students by controlling the dynamics of classroom discourse: 'the teacher takes turns at will, allocates turns to others, determines topics, interrupts and reallocates turns judged to be irrelevant to these topics, and provides a running commentary on what is being said and meant' (Thornborrow, 2002, p. 176).

Thornborrow's conclusions match up with earlier ideas, such as Mahony's (1985). Mahony understood teacher attention swayed towards the boys as indicative of prevailing societal attitudes, stemming from attitudes at large: that boys are privileged learners (as males are privileged participants in society) and that this privilege is evidenced in the way boys monopolize teacher attention. In Mahony's study, for every two boys asking questions there was only one girl (p. 30). Stanworth's (1981) work also explored gender divisions in classroom talk, and her conclusions also rested significantly on teacher control:

> The important point is not that girls are being 'discriminated against', in the sense of being graded more harshly or denied educational opportunities but that the classroom is a venue in which girls and boys, dependent upon a man (or woman) who has a considerable degree of power over their immediate comfort and long-term future, can hardly avoid becoming enmeshed in a process whereby 'normal' relationships between the sexes are being constantly defined. (p. 18)

The teacher's role in classroom discourse seems certainly of prime significance to language learning. Mahony went on to focus on and analyze the disproportionate amount of time allocated in favour of boys. Stanworth (1981) did too. She said:

> Studies which have involved protracted observation of a variety of classrooms have shown, almost invariably, that boys receive a disproportionate share of teachers' time and attention. High achieving boys

are in some studies a particularly favoured group, claiming more of their teachers' energies than either similarly performing girls, or than less successful pupils of either sex.   On the other hand, although girls are criticized at least as often as boys for academic mistakes, boys are far more often reprimanded for misconduct and, in some classrooms, these criticisms account for a large share of the extra attention directed at boys. (p. 18)

It has been well argued by both Stanworth (1981) and Mahony (1985) that the implicit message to students is that extra time given to male students may suggest (to both boys and girls) that boys are simply more interesting to the teacher:

... [B]y more frequently criticizing their male pupils, teachers may unwittingly reinforce the idea that the 'naughtiness' of boys is more interesting, more deserving, than the 'niceness' of girls. (Stanworth, p. 19)

In light of the possible extra attention paid to boys and the more dynamic talk between teachers and boys, there is the issue of girls' relative silence in these same classrooms.   Spender (1980b) explored the particular patterns of silence among females.   She said:

Before analyzing the reasons for female non-participation in verbal activities in the classroom it can be quite enlightening to take a closer look at the 'chattering female' stereotype to see the way it has been constructed and used. . . 'Silence gives the proper grace to women,' wrote Sophocles in Ajax and his sentiments are still echoed in today's image of the desirable woman. (p. 148)

Spender's work contributed to an understanding of some pupils' silent classroom participation.   She said:

Both sexes bring to the classroom the understanding that it is males who should 'have the floor' and females who should be dutiful and attentive listeners. . . Within educational institutions girls are quickly made aware that their talk is evaluated differently from the boys. (p. 149)

Her conclusions on the matter were strong:

The message delivered in educational institutions is loud and clear; it simply doesn't do for girls to talk like boys. Girls must be more refined, more discreet in their verbal behavior if they want approval from either the teacher, or the boys, in the classroom. (p. 150)

Female ESL students may also have received such messages that 'girls must be more refined' and it seems reasonable to suggest that, for some, their silence may be a deliberate or even reasonable response to being instructed into such silence from their culture or perhaps also by their (white) language teachers. One of the early pieces of classroom research to support this possibility is found in the work of Clarricoates (1978) where she suggested that, ultimately, 'teachers like teaching boys' (p. 151 in Spender, 1980). Spender explained this sentiment on the part of teachers:

When boys ask the right questions, it shows that they are bright; when girls ask them it shows they know what is expected of them. . . When classroom management is the over-riding concern of teachers—and there are many who contend that control is the major educational objective in the classroom—the passivity of girls can be seen as a desirable feature. (p. 152)

It may be a strong possibility, as evidenced in 1970 – 1980s research, that there may have been an implicit message that girls count less to teachers. This message could reinforce a negative self-image and lead to withdrawal from participation on the part of female students. Research has consistently suggested that boys in classrooms talk more, that boys exert more control over talk, and that boys interrupt more. (Such research includes the early feminist linguistic work of Zimmerman and West, 1975 and the more recent work of Coates, 1993.) Girls, then, are assumed to listen more and to be more supportive when they do talk, largely serving as audience to a dynamic largely owned by boys.

The intersubjectivity theoretical approach that I have used in understanding the classroom I explore in Part II sees that classrooms are pervasive language environments where students are dealing with language most of the time and where language use is a way to participate and belong. Within such contexts, the participants are created by relationships and the relationships also create the context and create the participants themselves; it is mutual—it is constructive. Arguably then, the classroom dialogues are, in many ways, the main educational process (this view was expressed as early as Dewey, 1938, and in Stubbs, 1976). An important way to determine how ESL girls may be coping in classrooms may be to observe their language use and their silence and to wonder about teaching methods (such as initiation/response/follow Up) as contributing to their classroom participation.

Findings on gender and language do not seem to vary much, even as the participants and context of the interaction vary regarding age, social class, ethnicity, level of schooling, subject matter, sex of the teacher and time of the study (1970s, 1980s, 1990s). In Kelly's research (1988 in Graddol and Swann, 1989), both female and male teachers tended to pay less attention to girls than to boys at all ages, in various socio-economic and ethnic groupings, and in all subjects. Also, girls received less behavioral criticism, fewer instructional contacts, fewer high-level questions and academic criticism, and slightly less praise than boys across the age ranges and in all subjects. There are some reports that teachers direct more open-ended questions at boys in the early years of schooling, and more yes/no questions at girls (Fichtelius, et al., 1980, in Graddol and Swann, 1989). It also appears that boys tend to be 'first in' to classroom discussions because of the teachers' own non-verbal cues, particularly their 'gaze-attention', and that this eye contact is important in systematically offering boys more opportunities for participation (Paechter, 1998; Swann, 1998). This possibility is explored specifically in the case study put forward in this book.

Girls may be systematically marginalized in general class discussions with their teachers. Arguably, such marginalization denies girls the opportunity to work through their ideas with language or to practice and experiment with spoken words. Walden and Walkerdine (1985 in Paechter) also argued that the

active, curious, exploratory Piagetian child on whom Western primary education is founded is in fact not neutral but male; girls are encouraged to be passive by teachers, who then interpret their reluctance to challenge their ideas as evidence that they lack intelligence' (in Paechter, p. 34).

It may, then, be that approaches in teaching 'gender' the classrooms through particular classroom methods which encourage boys to speak and girls to say less.

Linguistic space in classrooms

Such 'gendering' may be seen most obviously in the proportion of talk-time. Mahony's (1985) evidence is that there is a disproportionate amount of linguistic space allotted to males in classrooms and that this has an effect on the female classroom experience—ESL or not. Even if or when the attention paid to boys is negative, their very presence in the classroom claims more teacher time and focus (Stanworth, 1981; Crozier and Anstiss, 1995; Potts, 1996 in Paechter, 1998). Teachers' attempts to get boys to consent to their authority might be one reason they allow boys more control over physical space, teacher attention and lesson content (Paechter, 1998). But, with the growth in emphasis on the importance of student-centred learning, classroom talk is increasingly seen as central to the learning process, particularly in language education. If ESL girls are not given or do not claim adequate access to classroom talk, this must impact on their learning of English. It seems more than reasonable to suggest that language is a form of social practice (as discussed in Chapter 1). It follows then that the way language is used in language classrooms reflects and even prepares students for gender roles and inequalities in society at large. Also, a range of international research has persuasively demonstrated that the skill to speak effectively in public confers social and/or professional prestige and that this usually falls to the males in any given society (Jones and Mahony, 1989; Coates, 1993; Nichols, 1983, 1998; Irvine, 1995; Tannen, 1995; Holmes, 1998a; Baxter, 1999, 2002). So speaking up in class is not just important for the opportunity to engage with ideas or with the language: it signifies and creates important social power and legitimacy.

From the theoretical approach of intersubjectivity, inequality of talk-time in classrooms is not an incidental or minor feature of male or female tendencies in speech but a result of complex social processes of belonging in certain ways. Relationships may propel a consistent imbalance. The implications of such conditions point to the possibility of girls having less opportunity to speak and engage with ideas, perhaps having lower confidence as a result, and having less recognition of their presence or involvement in general. In the rapid exchange in classroom discussions of teacher-student talk, it is often the first student who responds by raising a hand or making eye contact who receives the attention of the class. Swann (1998) and others suggest that such responders are usually male. By engaging in such forms of privileged interaction, teaching methods are not only distancing those who may be less competitive or aggressive, but

also giving those who already excel in claiming the floor (usually boys) further
opportunities to do so.

An overview of feminist linguistics

Gender in the classroom has borrowed many ideas from the field of feminist
linguistics. The relationship between language use and the female experience
has been a source of much discussion and controversy for feminist linguists
(Spender, 1980, 1982; Cameron, 1992; 1995a; 1995b; Coates, 1993, 1996,
1998a). These discussions seem to settle mainly on the explanations of power
and success in society and the role of females as either victims of patriarchy or
as independent active agents of their own making—or if such roles are
socialized or innate. Language used by males and females (and how such use
might be similar or different) is central to these debates. Gender, of course, is
not the only variable that influences language use. Nevertheless, linguists as
well as education researchers have provided evidence to suggest that gender is a
significant variable in social roles and that it plays a significant part in
predicting and explaining certain speech acts that cut across other variables,
including ethnicity (Holmes, 1992, 1994, 1998a, 1998b). Linguistic patterns
that are systematically found to be used much more by one gender than the
other are likely to offer insights to ESL educators attempting to understand the
construction of language use as a way to better understand language learning
environments.

This book on the construction of speech and silence in language classrooms
asks several key questions of the feminist literature: Is there observable
difference in the way that boys and girls use and receive classroom talk in a
language classroom? If so, what are the differences? What might be the
explanations?

If girls and boys tend to have markedly different patterns in their use of
language, then these patterns may reflect the language patterns around them. If
teaching methods give little recognition to the possibility of gendered language
experiences and create unequal language opportunities for the students as a
result, if there is a marked difference in the use of linguistic space, then this
needs to be examined by language education.

Robin Lakoff's (1975) seminal text, *Language and Woman's Place*, is regarded
as a driving force in bringing feminist concerns to the fore in sociolinguistics
(Coates, 1993; Hall and Bucholtz, 1995; Talbot, 1998). Lakoff's work in the

mid 1970s generated a host of subsequent empirical research in search of evidence to support or discount Lakoff's claim: females use specific strategies in discourse that limit their power. Lakoff's contribution spawned enormous debates on the matter, in large part because her work was considered largely intuitive rather than empirical--her observations came from her own experiences rather than from more structured or 'rigorous' research.

Nevertheless, feminist linguists suggest that males and females use language in different ways and for different reasons and they attempt to explore possible explanations for the differences. There is the basic distinction in the literature between the terms 'sex' and 'gender': 'sex' referring to the biological category, which is usually fixed before birth, and 'gender' referring to the social category associated with certain behaviors and is considered to be constructed throughout life (Coates, 1996; Talbot, 1998). It is the 'non-fixed' quality of gender which chiefly concerns feminists—that gender may be socialized into being or socially constructed for certain purposes (Crawford, 1995). Assuming that gendered linguistic characteristics, such as *female speech strategies* (my term, Julé, 2003), are not fixed but rather develop through life experiences, then there is an implication that such socialization also happens in classrooms, including, of course, language classrooms. For a teacher, the possibility that gender may be even partly constructed in the day-to-day classroom experiences or that such gendering could have implications for learning, means that the process of constructing gender needs careful examination.

Various cultures and social groups have been examined in a search for a greater understanding of gender similarities and differences in speech (Spender, 1980a; Pauwels, 1998). Sexist language presents stereotypes of females and males, sometimes to the disadvantage of males, but more often to the disadvantage of females. This is seen universally. In English, Lakoff's (1975) early example of 'master' vs. 'mistress' and the unequal connotations which are believed to surround these terms make them different--and to the detriment of females. Also, because of their linguistic history, terms such as 'waitress' or 'actress' imply that the standard is male and that the variation is female (Coates, 1996; Cameron, 1998). Most languages have similar examples (Lakoff, 1975; Spender, 1980a).

There are those who explore such sexism within the English language itself (Spender, 1980a; Pauwells, 1998) and those who explore the overtly sexist ways that language has been used by both males and females in English-speaking cultures (Spender, 1980a; Swann and Graddol, 1995; Swann, 1998;

Cameron, 1995a). Other research has explored various meanings attached to the same linguistic structures (Fishman, 1983), while feminist linguists have continued to debate whether certain forms are used more often by one sex than the other (Mills, 1995). There also exists a range of views about the amount of personal choice speakers have when speaking (Spender, 1980a; Cameron, 1998; Pauwels, 1998).

Cross-cultural studies of gender and language also confirm that language plays a very diverse role in the social construction of gender in various communities. At the same time, studies of the interaction between gender and language confirm that the effects of socialization through language appear very early in children's lives and across all cultural groups (Corson, 1993; Wareing, 1994; Wareing and Thomas, 1999). For example, the styles of interaction that caregivers (such as parents and teachers) adopt with very young boys may contrast with the styles that they adopt with very young girls. Corson (1993) argued that such language used with very young children is linked to the child's gender and that this contributes to differences emerging very early in children's lives.

Ultimately, feminist linguists hope that attention to language may denaturalize an assumed male privilege and the patriarchal system that secures it, thus loosening gender roles for both males and females. Sexism is not only located in the content or meanings of specific words or phrases but can also be found in discourse and the meanings and communication created by speech styles or patterns in longer spoken texts and within conversations.

The fascination with what language reveals of society is not a feminist invention. The early work of anthropologist Sapir (1929) interpreted the role of language as potentially limiting or liberating one's experiences. It is this view that has been borrowed to some extent by feminist linguistics, but is generally seen as an over-simplification of language use. Feminist linguists have utilized elements of the Sapir-Whorf hypothesis by saying that females have been taught to speak a certain way which they describe as 'weak'. As a result of such speech patterns, females are assumed to have become as unassertive and insecure as they are made to sound (or as they choose to sound). In this way, language predicts or reveals life experience. But presenting speech as 'female' opens up an enormous debate. According to Cameron (1998), the question 'Can we make generalizations about female speech?' is no longer seen simply as 'the obvious question to ask' (p. 17). Even with research suggesting that it is possible to make empirically-based generalizations about female speech, society now understands that there are many various femininities, not one, and that they present differently in various contexts--even within the same person (Holmes, 1992; Talbot, 1998). However, for the moment at least, it would appear to be possible to defend a notion of gendered tendencies without claiming that the experiences of one female need be generalized to all females in all circumstances.

Earlier research in feminist linguistics tended to focus on mixed talk settings; that is, how males and females talk in circumstances involving both sexes and the phonological or syntactic structures that were more evident in use by one sex compared to the other (Labov, 1970; Gumperz, 1982). Work in the 1960s - 1970s appears to have drawn predominantly on an essentialist paradigm of gender. This view of gender categorized speakers primarily according to biological sex and used mainly quantitative methods to document the differences and generalizations. Later, researchers began to turn their attention to broader aspects of talk, such as the conversational strategies characteristic of male and female speakers in public contexts. More recently, researchers have begun to look at single-sex interaction to ask questions such as: How do speakers 'do gender'? Is gender 'performed' differently in single-sex groups? If so, why is this? (Coates, 1993). These changes in focus have been accompanied by shifts in methodological perspectives, with the more recent research tending to use more qualitative and ethnographic approaches.

As gender continues as a key variable in studied anthropology, education, and linguistics, so research has broadened to explore variation in the entire gamut of linguistic strategies by employing a variety of methods. Certainly most of the more recent studies in linguistic variation associated with gender admits to more of a 'tendency' rather than a 'generalization' regarding females or males and their use of certain forms—believing that certain patterns are not innately male or female, but tend to develop into patterns over time in particular speech communities for particular purposes (Jones, 1980; Graddol and Swann, 1987; Eckert, 1989, 1990; Eckert and McConnell-Ginet, 1992; Acker, 1994; Sadker and Sadker, 1994; Mahony, 1985; Cheshire, 1998; Eisikovis, 1998)

Arguably, feminist linguistics has become a major force within sociolinguistics and is a growing interest within language education because of the significant way that gender is understood to relate to notions of society and social dynamics. However, the diverse and often oppositional arguments adopted within the field of feminist linguistics reflect wide-ranging theories that appear at times to be contradictory (Coates, 1998a; Talbot, 1998).

Nevertheless, most feminists see that females and males have been treated differently in different contexts and, as a result, may live particularly gendered lives.

Gender tendencies in speech

In the attempt to examine 'female speech strategies' (Julé, 2003) in the construction of speech and silence in a language classroom, it is worthwhile to identify the early particulars that Lakoff (1975) identified and what she termed 'woman's language':

1 Women have more words that relate to their specific interests, like sewing;
2 Women use 'empty' adjectives like 'divine' or 'charming';
3 Women use rising intonation in declarative statements;
4 Women use more hedges, like 'kind of,' 'sort of,' and 'I guess';
5 Women use the intensifier 'so' more than men do, speaking in italics for emphasis;
6 Women use hypercorrect grammar and pronunciation (men drop their g's - such as 'gonna' while women tend to stay more correct);
7 Women use super-polite forms or euphemisms and are the 'repositories of tact';
8 Women do not tell jokes, nor do they understand them. Women have no sense of humour;
9 Women use direct quotes when describing speech;
10 Women use more tag questions. (p. 55)

Women also interrupt less often and use more back-channel support. Of course, these early ideas appear rather strange in light of the generation of feminism that followed, one that now sees femininity as far more complex and individual. However, Lakoff's work was founded on her belief that women lacked confidence and that this deficiency was revealed in their speech. Such a view of females as lacking in confidence was regarded as highly problematic even then and much more so today. Many feminist theorists and linguists have since gone searching for data that identified these self-deprecating features (particularly American popular writer, Tannen, 1989a, 1989b, 1990, 1994, 1995, as well as John Gray's, 2002, *Men are from Mars, Women are from Venus*, stem from this view). For example, O'Barr and Atkins's research (1981) analysed the speech of women as courtroom witnesses. Their data showed that the frequency of 'women's language' did not necessarily correlate with gender but rather with social class and, in their case, courtroom experience. As such, O'Barr and Atkins suggested that women's language has been interpreted as 'powerless' language, but that such language patterns are not gender specific but power specific. However, in turn, their conclusions seemed contradictory in that they persisted in seeing female use of language as weak even though this 'weakness' could be compensated for by experience or by social status.

Coates (1993, 1996, 1998a, 1998b) discusses their research and others like it, such as West (1984) and Woods (1989), and suggests otherwise: that, regardless of social class or experience, it is gender that provides the point of reference regarding power in conversations. In her view, gender may be the prime variable in speech production, transcending all other variables.

Empirical data on gendered speech can work to dispel misconceptions and stereotypes of female speech, such as the myth that women talk more than men do. Some believe that there are no real 'sex differences' in speech at all because the core of discourse is always about who has the power and that this power could be unique and specific to each setting. If boys have the power, then they can dominate discourse; but if girls have the power, then they dominate discourse too. But feminism sees power as usually patriarchal and therefore rarely giving way to female power, except in certain circumstances and with specific training. In Lakoff's early work, she called for a 'relearning of language,' that females should recognize those speech patterns that undermine power, throw off their 'learned helplessness', and simply speak more like men. However, there is no empirical evidence to suggest that if females used more interruptions, for example, that this would dismantle patriarchy or create female power. The day-to-day experiences are too complicated for such simplistic self-help directives (Talbot, 1998).

Coates (1993) is exhaustive in her own identification and analysis of female speech patterns, particularly gossip (also explored in Jones, 1980). Coates's work specifically identifies categories which apply to forms of talk. She selected certain categories as relevant to a discussion of gender and language. Such linguistic features in her research are: topic and topic introduction; latching; minimal response; hedging; questions; and turn-taking. The features that she identifies are underpinned by her belief that female speech is not weak but rather often based on a goal of 'maintenance of good social relationships' (p. 139). Coates goes on to state that certain conversational settings might require varying levels of competition over relationship-building speech patterns for both males and females.   Regardless of setting, however, female conversations may more often be relationship/community based but surely 'the ideal (androgynous) speaker would be competent in both [settings]' (p. 139).

My research has attempted to identify particular patterns of gendered speech in a language classroom. Some need further discussion:

Hesitation

Back channel support is the verbal and non-verbal feedback listeners give to speakers. Listeners can give feedback by saying things like 'mmm,' 'uhuh,' 'yeah,' and by nodding, smiling, frowning, and by other body language including gestures and body posture. That such a feature may be more typical in female speakers has been reported in the research of Zimmerman and West (1975); Fishman (1983), and discussed rigorously in the work of Coates (1993). A listener not giving back channel support is usually reported as making a female speaker feel unsure of herself, and can lead to her hesitating, repeating herself and sometimes ceasing to speak entirely.

Hedges are linguistic forms which dilute an assertion; for example: 'sort of,' 'like,' 'I think,' 'kind of.' Hedges indicate explicitly the speaker's attitude towards their utterance. For example, 'should', 'would', 'could', 'may', 'might' (all modal verbs) can be used to indicate that a speaker does not want to sound completely certain about something. Other words included here are: 'perhaps', 'really', 'quite', 'maybe'.

Studies suggest that women use hedges and modal forms more than men, although the underlying reasons are disputed. Lakoff (1975) claimed it was because women may be less confident than men and more nervous about asserting anything too strongly. But other studies (discussed largely by Coates, 1993) claim that women want to create a sense of community (and have reasons to do so) and use forms which, by being less direct, allow for disagreement without any explicit confrontation. Perhaps the use of hedging devices is connected to a female sense of community building and inclusion and is part maternal (Wareing, 1994).

Interruption

Some research suggests that male speakers interrupt female speakers more than they interrupt other male speakers, more than females interrupt males, and more than females interrupt other females (Zimmerman and West, 1975;

Talbot, 1998). The findings that males are apparently biased in terms of their predilection for interruption with regard to women is assumed to indicate that such men act as if they have more right than women to speak in mixed sex conversations, and, conversely, that women act as if they had less right to speak than men in similar situations. The research in this area also reports that females, particularly in single sex conversations, are more likely to overlap rather than interupt one another's talk than males are (Spender, 1980; Coates, 1993).

Holding the floor

Another way that women's and men's conversations appear to vary is in the topics that they choose to discuss and the way they 'hold' the conversations to these topics. Women are reported as selecting more personal topics: their families and their emotions. Men, on the other hand, are said to prefer more impersonal topics, often based on factual or technical knowledge, such as sports or cars. Male topics have been found to require fewer intimate revelations, and also to emphasize the exchange of information as the basis for the conversation. Such topics in mixed groups tend to 'hold the floor' for longer periods. Women's speech in similar groupings, focus more on the development and maintenance of the relationship between speakers, fostered by an exchange of more intimate details and more supportive listening (Coates, 1993, 1996). With their topics, there is less 'holding the floor' and more male interruptions.

Silence as a female speech strategy

The particular feature of silence is distinct from the identification and examination of distinctive tendencies in female speech. Goldberger (1997) reports that 'silence is an issue not just for a subset of women... but is a common experience, albeit with a host of both positive and negative connotations' (p. 254). Silence in female speech was not identified in the early work of Lakoff (1975) but has become a significant part of her more recent ideas (Lakoff, 1995). She mildly defended her early omission as 'not really surprising. It is easier to perceive what is there as meaningful, as opposed to discerning meaning in the absence of a phenomenon' (p.25).

Silence is defined as the absence of speech and, therefore, can potentially be complicated to identify in transcription work. It can be, by comparison, relatively straightforward to interpret speech strategies (if they exist). Silence is more ambiguous and can only be understood by an interpretation of context. Lakoff (1995) admits that not all silence is necessarily about power, but she advises that researchers should consider this possibility. She particularly isolates two of her women's speech patterns as related to silence: lack of interruption and lack of topic control (cf. West and Zimmerman, 1983; 1987). Lakoff suggested that if one is interrupted, then, in a sense, one is silenced by being stopped.

Gal (1991) was clearer than Lakoff that there is a big difference between self-imposed silence and externally imposed silence, though such a distinction may be difficult to perceive from the outside. There is evidence to suggest that a sense of feeling silenced and of feeling unheard are painful and frustrating experiences and that these experiences may apply to many females. It has been suggested that to be ignored when speaking is the equivalent of being told that you know nothing or have nothing to say worth hearing. Lakoff (1995) believed that the male ignoring of female speech, such as not offering eye contact or a sound of recognition, is a powerful way of silencing the speaker.

Zimmerman and West (1975) reported that the length of silences by both male and female participants when in mixed sex settings was three times as long as in single-sex settings (1.35 second in single-sex setting, but 3.21 in mixed-sex settings). Minimal responses (hmmm, uh huh) were offered by males in mixed-sex settings, but only after a length of silence. Such a delay may indicate a lack of significance to the (female) speaker. Previous research by Zimmerman and West (1975) and Fishman (1983) pointed to the listener as an active participant even when the listener is completely silent. But if the silent listener is male, his silence seems to indicate his lack of interest; while if the silent listener is female, it may indicate her lack of significance. It has been argued that control is often subtly achieved by nonresponse, and nonresponse is not infrequent in classrooms 'when a female student raises her hand and is recognized, her comment often receives no response' (Lakoff, 1995, p. 28).

Furthermore, the opportunities for silence or talk are related to teacher-pupil behavior. For example, if teachers generally talk more than 70 per cent of the time (a result found in Stubbs, 1976), then there will only be a small proportion of time available for pupil response and participation through speech. The recognition of silence as an element of speech may be crucial in understanding of language classrooms. Silence has been used to legitimate the view that indicates that female pupils may see themselves as relatively mindless or invisible. Girls and women who have emerged from relative silence in a particular context reveal that their silences have been a way of surviving in what they experienced as a dangerous or hostile environment (Gal, 1991; Goldberger, 1997). Silent girls may be revealing hints of their isolation, their lack of belonging, or their acceptance of a status quo.

Silence may or may not be a conscious strategy on the part of females. Coates (1993) identifies silence as part of her discussion of the societal perception of female 'verbosity' and the cultural requirement for females to say less. She cites Soskin and John's (1963) study that found it was men who took longer to describe a picture (average thirteen minutes) as compared to women (average three minutes); and that males took up to four times the 'linguistic space' in most circumstances most of the time. Coates suggests that the myth of females as talkative leads to certain expectations of who has the right to talk. Here she agrees with Spender's (1980a) earlier hypothesis that female speech is viewed as 'chatter' or trivial and points to the view that seems to be shared by both males and females that what men do or say is important and what women do or say is less so.

Much sociolinguistic research has been carried out in many different situations in a search for the nature and underlying basis for gendered speech and much has been found to solidify the claim that females and males may use language differently or that their speech may be interpreted differently, even if or when the same speech strategies are used (Crawford, 1995; Hall and Bucholtz, 1995; Wodak, 1997; Talbot, 1998). Much of the research has given evidence that many folklinguistic beliefs about gendered language are false (such as a belief that females talk more than men). Also, the examination of male/female differences may be complicated by context, by power, and by interpretation of the very same linguistic forms. Nonetheless, certainly some differences appear with regularity across cultures and across social groups (Corson, 1993; Holmes, 1998).

Possible explanations for gender tendencies in language use

Much research and academic debate has been invested in discussing the possible reasons why there are gender differences in language use. Here, I have organized the three dominant explanations as socialization models, which I will explain; and I offer some support to those who hold more to the current constructionist explanation.

The socialization models: deficit, dominance, and difference

In the three common models of explanation for gender differences in language use discussed here, society is seen as responsible for the 'socialization' of gender roles: The Deficit Model; The Dominance Model; and The Difference Model.

The 1970s' *Deficit Model* of gender differences in Lakoff's work (1975) regarded females as disadvantaged speakers because of their use of language and suggested that this disadvantage could be responded to by females themselves.   She saw underlying social inequalities as rendering females inadequate in expressing their thoughts, their ideas, or even their needs. Women were deficient speakers.   Lakoff's argument was that, though some men may display these same strategies, 'weak' speech strategies are more representative of a women's place in society: in other words, that females have no 'real-world' power and their speech necessarily reflects this (p. 57).

Lakoff defended her ideas by suggesting that these differences are not as noticeable in academic women and that explains why so many female academics criticized her views; they failed to see her point.   But this defense only served to undermine her view that women spoke in 'weak ways'. She insisted that female speech strategies are present in the general population and that such identifications of them could be understood as helpful to women in making 'stronger' linguistic choices.   Her claim was that women characteristically use a speech style that is hesitant, ingratiating, and weak and that women are 'deficient' in language use.   But Lakoff's claim was oversimplified because her study of isolated variables demanded further explanation of such variables as the context, the setting, and the topic.   In fact, results of the empirical work done since make it impossible to conclude, with any confidence, that Lakoff's nine features of female speech are indeed the norm for most women in most situations.

However, some feminist linguists agreed with Lakoff in seeing the inherent sexism in language use as determining the subordination of females in any conversation.   As a result, in small groups or in classroom talk, girls are believed to be systematically disadvantaged and to collude in their own disenfranchisement by speaking in 'female' ways.   Spender (1980a) saw that the subordination of females may be sustained through their own language strategies and that it maybe women themselves who unwittingly collude in their own 'deficiency'.   Assertiveness Training courses were seen as possible solutions, but such programs failed to generate the desired results.

The Dominance Model of gender differences is closely related to the Deficit Model and refers to the work of researchers who claim male privilege is manifest in recurring speech patterns. Those who work (or worked) with a Dominance Model emphasize the need to challenge a perceived underlying social dominance of men over women in speech. They believe that there cannot be a simple checklist itemizing male and female language on the basis of linguistic forms, because a single linguistic feature can function in different ways according to the context of interaction and according to the speaker. In the Dominance explanation, there is a shift away from the itemization of linguistic features that characterize the Deficit Model to an examination of the dynamics of interaction.

In the Dominance view, attention to language is not carried out with a view to solving the social inequities surrounding all discourse. Doing away with tag questions, for example, cannot bring an end to patriarchy; this is too simplistic. The problem then is not 'male' or 'female' language patterns themselves but male power or privilege in social structures which is unchallenged: language use reflects social power. In the Dominance explanation, attention to language can denaturalize the patriarchy and allow female speech patterns into that power (i.e. that women's speech is not 'deficit' in and of itself). Part of the desilencing of women was to recognize that when women use distinctive speech patterns, these patterns may well be highly adaptive and necessary (Coates, 1996).

An example of Dominance research is the work of Fishman (1983) who examined the number of questions females ask during conversations. Fishman found that, out of 370 questions posed in male/female conversations, 263 were asked by women. Fishman understood such an imbalance as signifying that females were trying to ensure male attention by posing questions. Fishman interpreted such results as alluding to male power: that females need to serve the role of 'asker' to participate in a conversation. The fact that a similar strategy may be engaged in by men would be interpreted differently and this different interpretation points to the fact that men are the points of reference within most social interactions. Males use dominance strategies (such as interruptions), whereas females use supportive strategies (such as minimal responses). In a Dominance Model, both roles are exercised in the interests of the male.

However, the *Difference Model* of gender differences in language use regards all language as valid. In this view, individuals are not regarded as responsible for the ideological meanings in the language they use; they simply use them. Power relations in society are not seen as the main motivator for certain speech patterns. Individuals apply their own assumptions to discourse and the patterns themselves are seen as benign (Gumperz, 1982).

Most significantly, this approach has been adopted by Tannen (1989a, 1989b, 1990, 1994, 1995, 1998) who has examined gendered linguistic styles in various contexts but primarily in intimate relationships. Her work has received a wide and popular readership, particularly in North America. Tannen, a student of Lakoff, extensively explored and explores gender-related differences in conversational style, though her work is viewed as superficial by many feminist linguists (including Cameron, 1998; Coates, 1998a; Troemel-Ploetz, 1998). Tannen argues that gendered speech differences exist because of differences in 'gender culture'. She believes that the 'effect of dominance is not always the result of an intention to dominate' (p.10)—that males do not intend to hold such power.

She offers little critique of such dominance (seeing power as neutral) and this omission in her work is debated and divisive in the field of Applied Linguistics. Whether power is intentional or not, her critics see elements of power figuring in any analysis of spoken language and a force that cannot be ignored or dismissed as irrelevant. A fundamental principle in Tannen's view is a 'soft' understanding of social construction. She believes that roles are created (not given) in interaction; that the context is created (not given) by talk and action; that nothing that is said is the single doing of one person but is communal; and finally, that there are neutrally distinct gendered linguistic features. Tannen asserts that language cannot be arbitrarily aligned by political/power issues because it only has meaning within each community or relationship—it is 'too contextual' to assert any generalities to power or subservience. For Tannen, the two sexes are simply different and, as a result of such neutral but significant difference, males and females cannot easily understand each other. Tannen's books are directed to her largely female readership to help with a needed understanding between the sexes.

This view of difference, and what Tannen does with it in particular, is attractive to some because of its rejection of blame on individual users of language. It claims women are not responsible for their 'weak' style of speech, and men are not responsible for dominating conversations. It is just the way things are. However, Tannen fails to make clear that, even if male and female ways of talking are simply different, her work does imply blame on the part of women (they should be more understanding). As a result, she has been accused of creating a genre of self-help material aimed solely at females, perpetrating the view that, when there is lack of relationship, it is the females who need to adjust (Troemel-Ploetz, 1998). This appears to me to be a valid criticism of the Difference Model in general: it is associated with a political stance while proclaiming it has none. Tannen believes that there is no deliberate male dominance in speech acts and that any discrepancies in legitimacy are neutral ones. And yet she sees it as the role of women to create good communication between the genders. In addition to this, Tannen is not very clear concerning the role of ethnicity (or other variables such as age, social class, and religion). If males and females come from two different 'cultures,' then there is a lack of clarity as to how ethnicity figures into such 'gender wars'.

The constructionist explanation

Though the complexities of Deficit, Dominance, Difference Models are far more far-reaching than I have explored, it may be sufficient to say that all three models of explanation share a basic acceptance of gender differences in language use as often socialized differences (created by social pressures and social realities). These three explanations are the main ways in which language and gender have been explained for the last twenty-five years. All, to varying degrees, have their roots in theories of acculturation or socialization and not genetic determinism. However, the recent work of Crawford (1995), Cameron (2001), and Baxter (2002) suggests a slightly different emphasis on understanding gender differences: that of construction rather than socialization. In their views, one's identity is a collective of 'situations and events' (Cameron, 2001, p. 48). Such 'situations and events' could transcend generalized gender differences, and be made evident in one's own particular language use and one's own active choice in one's behavior.

The particular use of intersubjectivity as the theoretical basis for my work here suggests that I too hold to a more constructionist view of gender and language use.

Constructionist theories can be, and are, applied to a whole number of fields, whereas deficit, difference, and dominance are specific to the field of language and gender. All three see gender as somewhat fixed (able to be generalized), whatever the reasons; and that gender remains basically fixed unless through political or educational intervention. According to Baxter (2002), a constructionist theory focuses on the relationship between speakers and the social world and the role of the speakers' own agency to 'do gender' each and every time they speak. People have choice and power. Both constructionism and the theory of intersubjectivity are about the need to continually negotiate oneself with others; identity is, therefore, never fixed, always in process, and always negotiable.

I see that speech and silence may well be constructed in language classrooms, believing that each student may behave differently in different contexts, with different 'situations and events'. Within the constructionist view, one's participation is developed through the recognition, or lack of it, in the context as a point of reference to one's own place of belonging (intersubjectivity). But each student also acts upon the classroom language; that is, each is active in the continual process of negotiation. My use of an intersubjective approach to understanding the speech and silence in language classrooms is a slight departure from the three more established feminist explanations for gender differences in language use: the Deficit, Dominance, Difference Models. Though I do not minimize the role of socialization in creating speech tendencies, the data from the classroom I observed has convinced me that, in speech patterns and particularly in silence, the girls have been constructed by the 'situations and events' in the language classroom itself and have also individually participated in constructing them.

Why any differences would matter anyway

Many studies have used various methods to find out whether males and females speak differently. I see the Deficit/ Dominance/ Difference perspectives as representing particular eras in feminism (perhaps particular eras of multiculturalism as well), ranging from initial outrage to almost an acceptance and certainty of the existence of speech tendencies. Most discussions of sex-role/gender socialization have been based on the premise that differences are greatest in adults (like Lakoff's early set of identifiers), and this follows from the idea that differences are socialized into being and are created over time (Swann, 1998).

What can be learned, then, in this discussion of the feminist language debates of difference? Feminist debates about difference and dominance, or that perhaps difference *is* dominance, or even my alignment with the constructionist model, do not answer the proverbial 'so what?'. If girls use hedges or tag questions or more silence in speech, then it is surely the strategy's significance and not its existence that needs to be reviewed. Also, social relationships and power or lack of power influence what is being said. An examination of classroom talk is, therefore, an important response to the issue of why differences matter: because language use can reveal learning. It is true that if a female ESL student says very little, she could simply be shy; however, she could be silenced and marginalized and constructed to be quiet by the 'events' around her. Her silence could be a product of socialization: her culture, her gender roles, her teacher, the educational system in general, the particular school community, or a combination of all of these. Or her silence could be also something that she has constructed into place for her own reasons.

Gender is regarded as a prime linguistic variable influencing one's speech experiences. Various descriptions of researched differences and the various explanations by feminist pedagogy and feminist linguistics have been put forward in this chapter. Also, the powerful ways gender impacts upon the educational experience have been discussed, with particular reference to the issues of 'teacher talk' and use of 'linguistic space' that, in most studies, place girls at an educational disadvantage. Because a key factor in the language classroom experiences is spoken language, classrooms are often sites of linguistic struggle that reveal a struggle on the part of many girls. As such, the language classroom is a crucial research site in which to explore the way speech and silence are possibly constructed by participants. In addition to this, the particular marginalization of ethnicity within Canadian society makes the girls' position one of multiple marginalizations: they are girls and they are from a silenced ethnic group in Canada.

Gender and language is certainly a well-developed field in both Education as well as Linguistics. The findings in these areas, though complex and contradictory, could be said to settle on the basic view that male participants are the legitimate ones in large mixed groups in most societies (including the Punjabi community) most of the time. Add to this then the power of ethnicity and cultural values and the forces at work in language classrooms are compounded. Chapter 3 examines the particular role of ethnicity, specifically the 'visible' minority of Punjabi Sikhs in Canada, and what such language students would need in their language classrooms.

3

What a Language Student Needs

All students require the attention and care of their teacher as well as the teacher's basic competence concerning solid teaching methods, accurate formative and summative assessments, and a grasp of the curriculum content. However, language students have yet more particular needs. These needs may center around harmonizing the role of their home culture (their ethnicity) and their heritage language within their life as a student. What a language student needs from the language teacher is a meaningful recognition of the heritage language and home community as well as a grasp of language learning principles. Canadian language students (or language students in Canada) have particular local complexities to navigate. Some complexities are outlined here, along with influences on ESL education in Canada and current trends in teaching practice.

Heritage language education

According to Ashworth (1992) the maintenance of heritage languages for children in Canada has been foundational to the development of a Canadian multicultural framework (assuming that Canadians are committed to this) because any limiting of a minority language would limit an ethnic group's sense of self. She believes that understanding one's own ethnic group and language empowers students by validating their ethnic legacy and developing the ability, confidence, and motivation to succeed as people. In other words, heritage preservation creates a sense of personal identity and community belonging that is foundational in the educational experience (Cummins and Swain, 1986; Moll, 1992).

Toohey (1996b) also speaks of the benefits of heritage communities, though she questions if private schools along ethnic lines might be seen as a reaction to the problems in public schooling and wonders if the separation of heritage groups may construct an underclass in society where hybrid-like language patterns can separate, isolate and trap. However, Toohey believes that no primary-aged child enters school with a mastery of any language. If second language learners are wholly immersed in English mainstream classrooms, which may do little to recognize their diverse backgrounds, then this may mean the complete loss of a first language and, therefore, a loss of personal wholeness. Such loss of one's first language is known as 'subtractive' bilingualism (Norton, 1995).

Heritage language programs (known as HLPs) began in English Canada in the mid 1970s (as did compulsory French studies for English children) with much criticism because of the cost and financial burden placed on the school boards. Essentially any ethnic group could request an HLP and many did so as a way of protesting against compulsory French, mounting up costs far beyond expectations. These programs initially served as appendages to the regular school curriculum yet certain ethnic groups desired a more central and vital role for their languages. Such requests fueled local debates, revealing a prevalent attitude among mainstream Canadians that the idea of multiculturalism could be tolerated but, when increasing requests for minority schools continued, the goal of education ought to be one of Anglo-conformity, hence 'mainstream' public schools (McAndrew, 1987). In many ways, multicultural policies revealed the Anglo-bias of the Canadian public during the 1970s; such attitudes did and still do permeate Canadian education (Burnet, 1984; Cummins and Danesi, 1990).

In such a social climate, several ethnic groups across Canada established their own schools, taking advantage of the opportunity to choose to maintain their languages publicly and not simply as integration into mainstream Canada but as a centralising force for their group maintenance. Today, a few Ukrainian, German, Russian, and Punjabi schools are scattered across Canada and are supported in part by public money (Cummins and Danesi, 1990).

Punjabi Sikh education in America and Canada

In her exhaustive study of a group of Punjabi Sikh teenagers in California, Gibson (1988) stated that she believes that there are two key elements at work that may undermine success for the Punjabi Sikh communities in American society. The first is 'structural inequality,' which emphasizes the political and historical differences of Punjabi Sikh children and those of the Western mainstream (that is, that the history of these societies are too different from each other).

In response to the question 'Is it possible for a student to be accepted by non-Punjabis and Punjabis?' one girl in Gibson's study replied:

> 'A boy can and a girl can't. A girl can be willing to mix, but her parents must be willing to let her go out with American girls, at night or during the day, over to their house, have them come to our house. Our parents won't let this happen. Even my little sister—she's about ten years old—my parents don't want her to go next door to play with the neighbour's children. I can't mix with American kids. I'm ready to, but my parents won't let me. That's the whole thing.' (Gibson, 1988, p. 164)

Such complexities involving both gender and 'Punjabiness' may be a real issue for Punjabi girls in American schools. Gibson's notion of 'structural inequality' may help explain this dislocation by suggesting that the 'two' cultures are just too different.

The second major element of Gibson's analysis concerning Punjabi children in American schools was 'cultural discontinuity' which explains certain problems of Punjabi students in the state school settings as largely due to a 'mismatch' between the culture of the school and that of the students' home. Gibson's (1988) explanation of key tensions surrounding Punjabi Sikhs in the United States may be contrasted with a Canadian independent private school, in which the latter appears to have a greater 'match' of culture and language in the school setting. A sociocultural view of learning as being deeply embedded in community indicates that a culturally specific school (like an all Punjabi-Sikh one) could be effective by preventing a culture clash.

Gibson (1988) may agree. She said:

Punjabi children, both American-born and those who arrive in this country during their preschool years, do comparatively well in school and, by a number of different measures, are as successful in school as their majority-group classmates. [However,] all face substantial difficulties.... . All could do significantly better and enjoy their education much more were the barriers to their success eliminated or reduced. Newer arrivals, moreover, do far less well because the barriers in many cases simply prove too great to overcome. Some of these barriers lie beyond the purview of school officials, but others relate directly to matters of school policy and practice. (p.167)

Cummins and Swain (1986) claimed that conversational skills in a second language may take five to seven years of only school-based exposure rather than the two years it appears to take for a child to learn English in a more immersed, mainstream setting. And so one implication of Cummins and Swain's (1986) research is that, in the case study examined here, a language student's acquisition of English might be delayed because of the lack of other more fluent English speakers: she would take longer to become fluent in an all Punjabi classroom. On the other hand, if cultural discontinuity is a hurdle of the mainstream multicultural school settings (Gibson, 1988), then one could expect that this single culture school should also support the language learning experience because of the strength of a shared linguistic and ethnic community in the classroom. Culturally specific schooling may result in students needing a longer period of time to become fluent in a particular language, but the 'belonging' to a particular cultural group may have more significance to a student's overall development and may be worth the wait.

Punjabi Sikhs in Canada

In order to provide a fuller understanding of this language classroom context, I review pertinent details of Canadian immigrant history.

The permanent French and British settlements in Canada in the 16th century generated a bitter rivalry between the two ethnicities, including rivalry for language use. Their conflict also brought a marginalization of the local Aboriginal cultures. Global forces (such as the French and American revolutions) explain some of the continuous tensions that surrounded the initial French/English nature of Canada (Fleras and Elliott, 1992; Ghosh, 1996). The 'Westward Expansion' (settlement across the continent to the West Coast) occurred throughout the late 19th and early 20th centuries. Such settlement served to further complicate the Canadian colonial experience because ethnic groups other than French or English, such as the Ukrainians, the Germans, the Italians, and the Chinese, began to populate this vast country.

Canada's identity as a former colony shared by both France and England has increasingly been challenged by the significant numbers of people coming from other parts of the world—those of neither French nor English origin. The British North America Act (the BNA Act of 1867) proclaimed Canada as British, but the last quarter of the 20th century in particular witnessed Canada grappling with fundamental questions about its national identity, centering largely on its linguistic nature (Fitzpatrick, 1987; Ghosh, 1996; May, 1999). Canada became officially bilingual in 1969 as a political response to growing dissatisfaction within French Canada (Fleras and Elliott, 1992). However, tensions between the French and English populations have been a constant feature of Canadian life, with current French resentment expressed through separatist political will (McLeod, 1993). The latest Quebec referendum in 1995 asked Quebecers to vote on a separate state and 49% voted yes. Such a close vote unnerved the country; talk of a future referendum is a regular feature in Canadian politics and in Canadian cultural life (Fleras and Elliott, 1992; Ghosh, 1996).

However, a shifting population has led to growth in the English-speaking population over the declining French throughout most of Canada. The number of French speakers has narrowed from 29% to 24% in the past fifty years (*Statistics Canada*). Most French speakers reside in Quebec, but not all and not all Quebec residents are French. The most common nonofficial languages in Canada are Ukrainian, German, Italian, and Chinese respectively, with now only 1% of the population declaring an Aboriginal language as a first language (Cummins, 1985; Cummins and Swain, 1986; May, 2001). In an optimistic response to such complex linguistic diversity, Canada became the first country to adopt a multicultural policy in 1988, attempting to include all ethnic groups in developing a modern Canadian identity. And yet since then, as throughout its history, Canada has continued to struggle in its management of its linguistically and ethnically diverse population, particularly concerning education (Fitzpatrick, 1987; Fleras and Elliott, 1992; Ghosh, 1996; May, 2001). Such discussion of the Canadian identity is a part of understanding the social climate surrounding the Punjabi Sikh school in this study.

There are currently approximately 250,000 Sikhs in Canada and 140,000 of them live in British Columbia (*Statistics Canada*). This number makes British Columbia one of the largest concentrated area of Sikhs outside of India. For many Punjabi Sikhs, the suburban community in British Columbia is both a port of entry to Canada and a permanent home. Punjabi Sikhs first arrived in Canada by way of British Columbia around the time of England's occupation of the Punjab district of India during the Victorian era. There was considerable mobility, particularly surrounding the time of Queen Victoria's diamond Jubilee celebrations in 1867 when world travel opened up so that all parts of the British Empire could be represented at the celebrations in London. The Punjab's colonial relationship with England was considered peaceful, believed to be in large part due to the autonomy the British leaders allowed the Sikhs in exchange for their work in military service (Johnston, 1989).

By the turn of the last century, the British Empire appeared to welcome and encourage travel within its commonwealth areas. During this period, Punjabi Sikhs, particularly the soldiers (all male) of the Indian Imperial army, began to explore predominantly English-speaking countries such as Australia and Canada. Many of these men returned to the Punjab with stories of their travels, but many more remained abroad and settled, some sending money home to the Punjab for family or arranging for potential wives and family to join them (Jagpal, 1994).

Early immigrant experiences in Canada were often painful ones. Johnston (1989) explains that Punjabi settlers in Canada were 'isolated by their pattern of life as well as by language, culture, and the attitude of the host population' (p. 8). Both the Punjabis and their Canadian hosts expected the stay to be a temporary, economic one. The exclusion that surrounded and hounded them, particularly the denial of the vote in spite of their being British citizens and a direct-travel-only policy upon landing when no direct travel was actually available from India to Canada, virtually arrested immigration from India between 1908 and 1920 (Johnston, 1984; McLeod, 1989a, 1989b; Minhas, 1994).

A head tax and the general denial of entry for women (only nine women immigrated between 1904 and 1920) discouraged Sikh immigration. In 1914, the infamous *Komagata-Maru* incident in Vancouver harbour highlighted the tensions. *Komagata-Maru*, a ship carrying many family members of Punjabis already in British Columbia, arrived in Vancouver's harbour carrying over 300 Sikhs. It was forbidden to dock because of a fear of political enemies on board and, after several months of sitting in the harbour through a particularly hot, dry summer, the ship was escorted out to sea to travel back to India. By this point, however, several hundred Punjabis, who were already living in the surrounding Fraser Valley and employed at sawmills and lumber camps, were waiting for the arrival of friends and family. The action appeared cruel, though controversy still exists concerning possible political prisoners on the ship. Many of the early Punjabis lived and worked in British Columbia for over twenty years before their family members were eventually permitted to join them (Johnston, 1984).

The first Sikh temple was built in Vancouver in 1906 and is the oldest Sikh temple in North America. With the eventual arrival of wives and families, Punjabi Sikhs began to develop family agriculture projects (i.e. farms). Though many of the early Punjabis made great efforts to assimilate into the community by cutting their hair and wearing western clothes, others adhered to their traditional dress codes and endured racist taunting by the larger, mainly white, Canadian community as a result. By 1958, immigration policies were slowly beginning to change; by this time, the small Sikh community in Canada had already produced two or three generations.

Early twentieth century anti-Asian sentiments produced legislation that prohibited Punjabis from permanently owning land in British Columbia. It was not until 1967 that this legislation changed to allow immigration based on occupation or financial investment rather than being 'white'. By then, the Punjab itself had long been divided between Pakistan and India, since 1947, with many Sikhs uprooted and looking for a new home and a new security (McLeod, 1989a, 1989b). The connection of the Canadian Sikhs with the Punjab remained strong, in large part due to most Sikh men in Canada needing to travel back to India to court potential wives and to arrange marriages. Such practices remain strong even today (McLeod, 1989a, 1989b; Minhas, 1994; Angelo, 1997).

During the 1970s and 1980s, more and more Punjabi Sikhs settled in British Columbia. In spite of continuing racial tensions and growing resentment by white Canadians who believed that their jobs were being taken from them, Punjabi children became a significant part of local public schools with many language programs serving newly-arrived Punjabi students. Today, the Punjabi Sikh presence at the local universities, on city councils, and in high ranks of local business are significant indicators that Punjabis have become an integral part of Canadian society. For many Punjabi Canadians, the hundred years of

Sikh settlement in the community have been painful but also profitable with 'assimilation and accommodation' both continuing to exist (Ng, 1993; Minhas, 1994; Moodley, 1999).

Key characteristics of Sikhism are embedded within the religious, cultural, and linguistic nature of the Canadian Punjabi Sikh community. A Sikh is:

> any person who believes in God (Akal Purakh); the ten Gurus (Guru Nanak to Guru Gobind Singh); in *Sri Guru Granth Sahib* [the holy book], other writing of the ten Gurus and their teachings; in the Khalsa initiation ceremony instituted by the tenth Guru; and who does not believe in any other religious doctrine. (McLeod, 1989a, p. 60)

Sikhism was founded five hundred years ago in the northern Indian province of the Punjab and so Sikhism and Punjabi culture are uniquely paired and quite difficult to discuss separately (Cole and Sambhi, 1990). Guru Nanak, the first leader (guru), founded Sikhism in 1469. The Punjabi word, 'Sikh', means 'learner'; Nanak's philosophy stemmed from a social reform position of equality—a radical separation from the predominant Hindu caste system. Nine gurus followed Nanak with the last of these establishing a dedicated group of people called the 'Khalsa' to resist the persecution of the invading Moghuls in the 16th century. It is the Khalsa philosophy, stronger in certain groups, that is believed to give the Sikhs their strong group identity, an identity established in part by their adherence to the '5Ks':

> Kesh: uncut hair with head covering; Kanga: a small comb; Kara: a bangle; Kirpan: a ceremonial sword for self-defense; and Kacha: breeches (loose undergarment). (Jagpal, 1994, p. 15)

It is expected that baptized Sikh men wear turbans and do not cut their hair; Sikh women wear scarves and also do not cut their hair. Male Sikhs use the name 'Singh', meaning 'lion', as a middle name, and female Sikhs use the name 'Kaur', meaning 'princess'.

In the case examined here, the particular expression of Sikhism is a moderate rather than an orthodox one. In this it is unique. Some Sikh communities in the country are considered more 'fundamental' and are tied more tightly with the newer and often more aggressive Sikh extremists (Singh, 1980; Kapur, 1986; McLeod, 1989; Raj, 1991; Minhas, 1994; Bolan, 2000).

ESL/language education—an overview

There are essentially two language learning paradigms: language learning viewed as a developmental cognitive process and language learning viewed as a social and spoken process. For some, language learning research takes second language learning to be largely the acquisition of linguistic knowledge (Piaget, 1932; Chomsky, 1969). In contrast, other theories of language learning stem from more sociocultural perspectives and describe learning as primarily a social process whereby learners in a community participate with more or less experienced members in both the learning and the performance of language practices (Vygotsky, 1981; Lave and Wenger, 1991).

The field of language teaching has undergone many fluctuations and dramatic shifts in pedagogy over the years. The Grammar-Translation Approach, the Direct Approach, Audiolingualism, and Communicative Approach are a few of the major movements. Each approach represents a perspective of language learning ranging from little spoken use of English, such as in the Grammar-Translation Approach, to a gradual approximation of English for communication purposes, as in the Communicative Approach (Hymes, 1972), including particular ways of teaching such as Krashen's (1982/1995) Natural Approach.

The field of second language acquisition developed rapidly in the 1970s and 1980s as a specific sub-section of Applied Linguistics. Many studies emerged on the particular skills, motivations, interests, and local contexts of various ESL settings. The field includes specific work on ESL children (such as Ashworth, 1992); ESL adults (Haverson and Haynes, 1982; Haverson, 1986;); ESL writing (Iwataki, 1981; Kroll, 1982; Stern; 1983, Stern, 1985; Leki, 1990); ESL reading (Dubin and Olshtain, 1977, 1986, 1987, 1990); ESL speaking (Celce-Murcia, 1987); ESL for academic purposes (Elbow, 1973, 1985); and ESL lesson planning and testing (Cohen, 1980, 1984, 1987) as well as countless other themes.

Particular social relationships of teachers and students and between students and students have invited studies concerned with understanding the role of identity and community (Hall, 1990, 1992, 1996). From such research, ESL education and research have become firmly attached to issues of social construction, seeing the individual experience as deeply rooted in local contexts and relationships (Lave, 1988; Ochs, 1988; Hall, 1990, 1992, 1996; Moll, 1992; Day, 1999). As such, various characteristics or variables of any given ESL learner may be understood as part of a 'system of culturally constructed relations of power, produced and reproduced in interactions' (Gal, 1991, p. 176). The ESL student experience is currently understood as a 'positioning' and therefore intimately related to the personal relationships and local cultures, or 'communities of practice' (Hall, 1990; Lave and Wenger, 1991; Toohey, 2000). In this way, intersubjectivity seems a good theory to attach to language education.

In spite of growing interest in the field of ESL research, much of it interdisciplinary, surprisingly little work has been done connecting gender and ESL. In fact, of the over one hundred sources I examined, only six researchers explicitly deal with gender and ESL (Holmes, 1991, 1992, 1994, 1998; Oxford, 1993, 1994; Sunderland, 1994, 1995, 1998; Willett, 1996; Vandrick, 1999a, 1999b; Norton, 2000).

What a language student needs

There are certain conditions an ESL student needs in order to learn language in a language classroom. I believe these include:

1   A comfortable, low-stress environment;
2   Language that is purposeful and used for real learning tasks;
3   Activities that allow for a range of language functions;
4   Comprehensible teacher talk, including meaningful questioning techniques and one-on-one time;
5   Teacher talk that is challenging and meaningful;
6   Language activities that are structured so to be able to use the language being modeled;
7   Opportunities to work with peers in problem solving and collaborative learning situations; and
8   One's first language and culture clearly acknowledged by the teacher.

I also believe that at the root of all second language acquisition is speech: the ESL student needs to actually speak. Speech is also linked to literacy development as well as to the processes of thinking and learning, so support for language use is 'a major principle for language development' (Gibbons, p. 29). Vygotsky (1981) supported this view, 'The child's intellectual growth is contingent on his mastering the social means of thought, that is, language use' (p. 10).

Even if ESL children are given access to good models of language, exposure is not enough to develop language. Language students need to actually use the language they hear. In this regard, a language student needs an interactive classroom (Cummins, 1988). Such a classroom environment is important for a language student in that such children need to be active in their own learning of the language; they cannot just observe language. If a language classroom is too teacher-centred, a language student can actually 'learn to fail' simply because she (or he) may be 'expected to play a passive role and have very few opportunities to participate successfully' (Gibbons, p. 27).

Some types of activities seen in an interactive language classroom include: problem solving activities, information-sharing activities, rank-ordering activities, encoding and elimination activities, describing and drawing, describing and arranging, jigsaw pictures, matching games, sorting, sequencing, consolidation activities (Gibbons, 1998; Cooke, 1998). Such activities can create a classroom environment where language students have various types of access to and experience with language use.

Also, language students may need a longer wait time for responding as well as the use of open-ended questions to 'help with generating speech' (Chaudron, 1988, p. 126). Also necessary can be 'a silent period' (Krashen, 1982/1995), where a beginning language student may take several hours or weeks to begin to utter English sounds.

'Good' language teaching methods

Gibbons (1998) lists features of a supportive classroom that a teacher can provide for language learners. Good language teaching methods include:

1 Providing a comfortable learning environment:
   'Positive responses by teachers to children's first language and culture are important in enhancing learners' self-esteem and developing their confidence.' (p. 11)
2 Planning opportunities for meaningful interaction between peers:
   'The peer group is a powerful resource to the learner, providing a wide range of models of language use, and the need to communicate offers the learner a real motivation to use language.' (p. 11)
3 Providing and structuring opportunities for the ESL students to be problem solvers rather than information receivers:

'This will involve collaborative learning, where the children are given responsibility for some of their own or groups' learning' (p. 11)

4   Presenting models of language that are understandable as well as expressing new ways to create meaning;

5   Providing frequent opportunities for interaction between teacher and individual students:

'...The quality and quantity of personal interactions with the teacher become a major resource for children's language development.' (p. 11)

6   Providing modeling of various questions:

'The questions [ESL] teachers ask are an important way to create the situations where certain language patterns are likely to occur.' (p. 21). Such question types include: classifying, describing, evaluating, explaining, generalizing, inferring, predicting and hypothesizing, and recalling information (p. 23 – 25).

Good language teaching methods include a variety of question styles as well as visual clues, gestures, props, pictures, diagrams, use of the chalkboard to write down key new words, repeating new words, and teacher conferencing (Cooke, 1998). ESL teachers need to speak clearly and be careful not to overcorrect (Krashen, 1982/1995). In the ESL literature on feedback, error correction has many meanings—and the issue of correction is perhaps at the core of teacher-student interactions in ESL (Chaudron, 1998). Some, like Krashen (1982/1995), say that correction is never appropriate in language teaching because, though the teacher may intend to be performing an 'instructional act' that could benefit the language student's language development, the risk of discouraging language use is too high. Such correction runs a great risk of creating anxiety and inhibition. Most agree that, for a 'good' language teacher, error correction should not constitute a major proportion of the classroom. Good language teaching should focus energy on communication and interaction. Good language teaching utilizes the vast array of questioning strategies that are more helpful than correction for creating meaningful relationships. Good language teaching pays attention to the content and the timing of teacher talk and thereby creates opportunities for language use and language development (Chaudron, 1988).

Though there are long held assimilationist views surrounding immigration and language education in Canada (and most of the Western world), such views have shifted to increasing support for culturally specific settings or heritage language programs. The Punjabi Sikh community's history in Canada places a set of conditions on this particular group because of the societal forces that propelled a need for a private Punjabi school for this ethnic community in the first place.

It is the political, historic, and societal forces as well as the 'match' of language and culture in home and school that exist in this case study which might create an environment for young Punjabi Sikh Canadians to participate in the maintenance of their culture and to participate in a place of belonging. This maintenance of ethnic heritage mirrors back a specific cultural group identity and influences the perception and validation of ethnic heritage that may be lacking in Canadian society at large. Belonging to an Indo-Canadian Punjabi Sikh community may provide these students with an opportunity to locate themselves within a context. Complexities that surround the classroom community and the female Punjabi role in particular matter significantly in positioning this study of language classroom experiences.

A language classroom needs a particular type of support for its language learners. There need to be comprehensible input and a vast variety of language experiences, particularly the use of various types of questions. It is also important that a language learning classroom have low anxiety levels, and that it produces a warm and encouraging language environment so that ESL learners can feel safe in using the language they are hearing. Questions, wait-time, various activities, and a meaningful relationship between teacher and student (which includes ethnicity in the frame of reference) are fundamental features of a 'good' language classroom.

With an understanding of local history as well as a grasp of language learning conditions, language classrooms can be productive in developing the spoken use of English. Perhaps without an understanding or a failure to use appropriate and effective teacher strategies, language use in classrooms can stall: that is, some language students may retreat into silence. Part II examines the conditions of one such room.

Part II

A Case Study of One Room, One Voice

4

One Language Classroom

What is of special interest in the language classroom I visited and examined is that this language classroom is within a Canadian Punjabi Sikh school where all the students share their Punjabi Sikh heritage. Such a culturally specific classroom is unusual in Canada. Because of the unusual ethnic make-up of the classroom, such a site is useful in applying an intersubjective view of classroom dynamics as well as examining the effectiveness of certain teacher practices.

Assimilation or multiculturalism?

An assumption underpinning an assimilationist ideology of education in Canada is that children (including some Punjabi Sikh children) who enter school speaking a language other than English are best served by attendance in mainstream classes which include native English speakers. Assimilation is defined by Fleras and Elliott (1992):

> as ideological construct . . . a process for managing diversity whereby minorities are absorbed in the mainstream either through passive exposure, deliberate intent, or imposed government policy. (p. 313)

In assimilation, minority children are expected to 'disappear' from public view as distinct groups as part of their 'price of progress and personal prosperity' (p. 313). Assimilation is accomplished in schools through 'mainstreaming', though this works against an advance of multicultural or anti-racist approaches to the education of minority-language children (Cummins, 1983; Fleras and Elliott, 1992; Ghosh, 1996; Moodley, 1999; May, 2001). Mainstreaming, however, cannot simply be understood as the result of reactionary assimilationist policies. The practice of placing children whose first language is not English alongside English native speakers has also been recommended as a progressive way of teaching English because of the role of one's first language (Krashen, 1982/1995). In any event, many ESL children in Canadian classrooms are enrolled in English-medium mainstream classrooms and receive special instruction in English when necessary.

The prevailing attitude towards ethnic diversity in English Canada during the first part of the 1900s was that all ethnic groups should give up their own languages and cultures and become assimilated to the dominant British group. Canadian educators viewed rapid assimilation as necessary to 'eradicate students' first language (L1) in order to facilitate the learning of English and acquisition of Canadian values' (Cummins and Danesi, 1990, p. 10). Educational policies at this time sought to eliminate all memory of a 'foreign' language through the suppression of language groups.

Canada's assimilationist history has played a significant role in current educational policy, and beliefs from 1867 to 1950 about language development among minority students have not altered all that much. Assimilationist views held in the 1990s include the beliefs that bilingualism may be a distracting force in the educational development of minority children; that use of the heritage language in the home impedes children's learning of English and overall academic progress; and that heritage language and/or bilingual education involving heritage languages will retard children's academic progress (Cummins and Danesi, 1990; McLeod, 1993).

In any event, in the mid 1980s, the first Punjabi preschool was established in British Columbia, Canada, to help children learn English while still supporting their first language (MacNamee and White, 1985). What became clear in this preschool setting was that the young children needed no encouragement to speak English (which they heard in society at large) but were surprisingly very reluctant to speak Punjabi, their first language, even among themselves. MacNamee and White (1985) reported that such a discovery alarmed Punjabi parents who began to believe that their language and culture could be weakened by the surrounding English society, with television and the media seen as major cultural and linguistic forces. These parents began to feel that a

Punjabi school extending into high school was perhaps necessary as a way to protect the Punjabi language and community within Canada.

Increasingly, research for first language maintenance in ESL emerged and educators and linguists began to see cultural sites, such as the Punjabi kindergarten, as desirable, in large part because language maintenance appeared to increase, not decrease, the likelihood of language proficiency in English (Chomsky, 1968; Derrick, 1977; Cummins, 1985; de Houwer, 1990; Ashworth, 1992; Jay, 1995). The intimate relationships at home experienced in one's first language pointed to the notion that language is personal and paramount in one's overall development. Research, including Piaget's (1932) Cognitive Theory, began to support the cognitive and conceptual necessity of maintaining one's first language and the personal relationships using these languages for communication; such maintenance is currently viewed as a cognitive advantage. The increasingly accepted understanding that one's first language, such as Punjabi, provides a frame of reference to second language acquisition is now widely supported (Krashen and Terrell, 1983; Berry, 1991; Ashworth, 1992; Toohey, 1992; Cummins, 1996). Other research identifies cultural identity as having a strong influence on personal linguistic identification and development (Hall, 1992, 1996; Norton, 1997, 2000). This would certainly be supported by the theory of intersubjectivity.

This group

Regular news coverage of the Punjabi community in British Columbia has included jarring reports of temple stabbings, criminal investigations into the community's Punjabi Credit Union, and the recent arrest of British Columbia's Punjabi Sikh separatists concerning the Air India bombing off the coast of Ireland in 1985. Media reports of several assaults on young Punjabi Sikh women are also of great concern   (Bolan, 1999, 2000, 2001). A Punjabi Canadian recently became British Columbia's and Canada's first 'visible' minority premier. Why such a distinction fell on this particular group sparked much discussion, particularly in light of the fact that other ethnic groups have been in Canada much longer, such as the Chinese, the Blacks, and certainly the Aboriginal nations (*Vancouver Sun*, 1999; *Globe and Mail*, 2000). And yet, in spite of such a presence in Canadian society, the Punjabi community has had little representation in academic study, and the establishment of a Punjabi Sikh school in British Columbia has been largely ignored by educational researchers

(Brah, 1987; Cumming and Gill, 1992; Gupta and Umar, 1994; Alexander, 1996).

Corson (1993) understood that minority girls, in particular, often do not receive equal opportunities to speak, become more passive receivers of knowledge, and fit the image of 'quiet' that their teachers create for them (something that could be said of girls in general but more so with 'visible minority' girls). His data indicated that it is mainly a failure on the teachers' part to create appropriate discourse conditions that produces a reluctance or inability to speak in many female ESL students, including Punjabi girls.

In their study of Punjabi children in Britain, Biggs and Edwards (1991) reported that, while there were no differences in the patterns of interaction initiated by ethnic minority children themselves with their majority culture (white mainstream) teachers, there were significant differences in interaction by the teachers. The minority children sought out the teachers' attention in much the same way as other children but the teachers spent less quality time interacting with them. Biggs and Edwards' conclusion was that the reluctance to form a relationship was seen as resting with the teachers. This lack of a relationship within an intersubjective view, where relationships are seen as central to the learning experience, is an issue.

Usually Canadian descendants of European immigrants, especially those in the third and fourth generations, see themselves as 'the norm' and other groups as 'special,' 'particular' or 'deviant' (Jay, 1995). 'Canadians' do not see their own food, clothes, beliefs, values, music as distinctive—as 'the majority', they do not have a particular culture, but rather individual identities. However, those from non-European backgrounds are often more aware of their ethnicity. Also, male students do not tend to express the importance of their gender to their ethnicity or how growing up male has anything to do with their identity and yet female students in Jay's (1995) study did strongly identify with their gender and ethnicity. As a result, minority girls may certainly be doubly marked.

The few images of Punjabi Sikh femaleness that exist in Canadian society are primarily of non-sexual, passive, docile beings, if they are seen at all (Bannerji, 1993). Bannerji explained that the virtual absence of Punjabi Sikh women in the Canadian media is due to their lack of social power, and because Punjabi women 'are not seen as an aid to beauty [as in female power]' (p. 177). Bannerji said, the women who clean [airports], or work in their usual jobs in the factories of Canada are hardly associated in the Canadian mind with the world portrayed in . . . films. They are considered a pair of working hands. (p. 177)

Such absence of representation means that girls such as the girls in this classroom may live in 'a vacuum, in a state of constant facelessness' within Canadian society (Bannerji, 1993, p. 178). Bannerji's work explained this 'facelessness', citing Canada's colonial and imperial past as responsible, where white settlers in Canada who (more like Britons) played the favoured, powerful roles. This, combined with a similar colonial experience of India, has placed South Asian /Punjabi women at the 'lowest level in the scale of exploitation in Canada' (p. 179). As such, Punjabi Sikh females in Canada are far removed from public recognition—they are, in fact, an unseen visible minority.

Some researchers have argued that both feminism and education have concentrated on reflecting white, middle-class issues and, as a result, conceal the vast variety and diversity of female experiences (Brah, 1987; Kothandaraman, 1992; Bhatti, 1995; and Amos and Parmar, 1984; Jayawandera, 1986 in Bhopal, 1997). Viewing a Punjabi experience only as 'exotic' leads to simplistic and limiting generalizations, and some studies have identified the same stereotypical perceptions of Punjabi girls in classrooms as quiet, docile, passive that are held by mainstream 'white' Canadians (Driver, 1977; Bhopal, 1997). Bannerji (1993) unpacked the notion of 'visible' minorities, attacking such a term itself as racist—are not all people 'visible', whites included? She went on to question what 'visible minority' implicitly means and how Punjabi Sikh girls are meant to feel about themselves within Canadian society:

This category of 'visibility,' and the construction of one's self as a 'minority' (a suffered member of society, even though a citizen and socially productive), are ways of rendering people powerless and vulnerable. They work as operative categories not because they possess any truth, but because they enforce the racist and imperialist relations which are already in place. They are injunctions, or codes of command, which bid us to be silent, to remove ourselves from areas or places where we may be seen. To be labeled 'visible' is to be told to become invisible, to 'get lost'. (Bannerji, 1993, p. 182-183)

Her argument is developed in more detail as follows; she said:

> Since we have already been allocated a space in the lowest level basement of
> Canadian society, it is entirely appropriate that we are visually and socially
> invisible. This invisibility is physical as well as geographical. Many
> researchers have shown, for example, that South Asian women are generally
> found in factories which are farthest away from dense population centres,
> working in areas with almost no transportation, in the lowest or the inner-
> most part of the factories. Even as white-collar workers, they tend to be put
> in jobs that do not demand much public contact. This is the analogue, in
> practice, to our visual absence for the social space. (p. 179)

Brah and Minhas (1985) also highlighted the social position of Asian women
'within the lowest rungs of class hierarchy in Britain' (p. 15) and suggest that
Canada, as a former colony of Britain, inherited certain attitudes toward
minority females. They also explain the patterns of settlement, the type of
mainstream, 'multicultural' schooling Punjabi children receive, and the kind of
jobs such minority children expect, girls in particular (cf. Brah, 1987).

Brah and Minhas (1985) analysed a (London) *Times Educational Supplement*
series of articles in 1984 focused on 'Asian' girls, entitled 'Walking the Tight-
Rope Between Two Cultures', which reinforced stereotypes of Punjabi girls.
Interpretive paradigms as 'between two cultures' and 'identity crisis' insist that
girls of Indian descent have a different experience from 'British' girls and fail to
account for the fact that many adolescent tensions are developmental and
universal. The ideological assertion of most things 'Western' as superior to
things 'Eastern' is achieved through expressions of sympathy for the girls
arriving home from school and 'changing from school uniform to Shalwar
Kameez (the traditional dress of the Punjab), from English to Punjabi, and
from noisy self-expression to a more subdued form of behavior' (TES). Such
assumptions, including the implicit suggestion that white girls are having
peaceful and vibrant experiences at both school and home, are examples of the
simplistic views regarding Punjabi girls that predominate in Western societies,
like Canada.

Brah and Minhas discussed several other stereotypes of Punjabi girls in school
at the time as being seen as 'passive' or 'docile'. In one case a teacher stated
that 'she could not tell one Asian girl from another in her class . . . and that it
didn't matter, so long as they were quiet' (p. 19). Other teachers in their study

reported Punjabi girls as rarely participating in class discussions saying they are 'shy, quiet, lacking in self-confidence, but well behaved' (p. 20).

Stereotypes in the schools they researched include images of Punjabi girls as 'exotic' or 'ugly', 'smelly', 'oily-haired', 'wearing baggy trousers' 'Pakis' (p. 20). Brah and Minhas suggest teachers 'need to break away from a narrow Euro-centric mode of thinking . . . which contributes to the devaluation of [other] experience' (p. 25). But simply saying that racism and sexism are alive and well did not and does not go far enough in explaining how Punjabi pupils, particularly girls, are positioned as marginal learners in their own classrooms.

In summary, Brah and Minhas's (1985) research revealed that when teachers addressed sexism as problematic, they ceased to evaluate racism; instead, they appeared to choose between the two phenomena, ignoring power differences between white and non-white girls. Teachers may also have adopted a pathological model of the ethnic family without understanding non-Anglo-American values. Simplistic attitudes among teachers in Brah and Minhas's eighteen year old study, especially that Punjabi girls are seen as repressed by a strange, male-dominated culture, undermine the complexity of such girls in classrooms (also see Bulbeck, 1998, for a further deconstruction of the non-western woman).

Being a Punjabi girl

Bannerji's (1993, 2000) research on Punjabi women in Canada articulates the issue of current Canadian attitudes surrounding female Punjabi ethnicity:

> [The Punjabis'] social location of here and now was developed through the long history of colonialism and imperialism in which white settler colonies like Canada played subordinate but favoured roles. The economy still continues along the same imperialist path, and its long worked-up justificatory ideology of racism still continues to be the important ideological force. This, combined with the neo-colonial nature of the South Asian countries, ensures South Asian women [their] place on the lowest level in the scale of exploitation in Canada. (1993, p. 178-9)

Stereotypes concerning Punjabis, including Punjabi females, have been explored in some academic discussions (Brah and Minhas, 1985; Deh, 1986; Bhopal, 1997). Angelo (1997) attempted to dismantle some of the strongest stereotypes of Punjabi females as silent and/or repressed. Angelo put forward an exhaustive description of a Sikh community in New York and used his anthropological study to challenge mainstream beliefs concerning Punjabi females. He said:

> The traditional submissive and reproductive image of the Indian female which has historically been promoted has never been the norm toward which the Sikh community has subscribed. The critical role of the Indian woman in society is further enhanced by the increased stature given to women in the Sikh tradition. Although customary practices and attitudes towards the woman's role continue to persist, the Sikh historical perception of the female role has generally been more enlightened than the Hindu or Muslim model. … The effect of the host culture's historic attitude toward gender in terms of equality was a powerful factor in affecting the extent of acculturation within the local community. Equal opportunity for educational advancement is and has been a salient feature of Sikh practice. The high degree of educational attainment, that is, 92 per cent of female respondents in possession of at least a B.A., attests to the relative equality of status of the Sikh female. (p. 169)

The role of women is different in the Sikh tradition from other Indian models in that the Sikh perception of the female is said to be more equal to male than in the Hindu model. Equal opportunity in education is a stronger feature in Sikh communities than in Hindu-Indian groups. 'The Sikh community in India has historically rejected the idea of women being considered inferior members of society, kept in subjection for the pleasure and purposes of males' (Angelo, 1997, p. 170), though importance is attached to women maintaining the values and traditions of the Sikh community with 'immoral' or 'irresponsible' behavior in a woman regarded as much more serious than in a man. Although no woman has ever been considered a 'guru', legends of women form an important element in Sikh tradition, often as temptresses, but not always. Strong and wise images of females do exist in much Sikh folklore. However, in spite of religious and social recognition granted to Punjabi Sikh women, Punjabi females do not necessarily experience freedom as it is understood in the West. Angelo explains:

> The relative ease with which the woman's role has expanded solely from being a reproductive, child-rearing homemaker was due partially to

traditional Sikh values and attitudes. Sikh females both in religious doctrine as well as in communal practice have been treated far more as equals to men than most other women in India. Although full equality in the Punjab is not in effect, their treatment as an inherent inferior is not recognized either. (p. 210)

In addition to the contradictions within the Punjabi Sikh female experience, the culture of the Punjab has not traditionally recognized a specific youth culture—some girls in India finish school as early as ten years of age to prepare for marriage, though an educated girl can obtain a better arranged marriage. From this point, education is seen as a worthwhile venture. Punjabi females are considered to have reasonable freedom of choice and behavior, though the roles of females in India and Indian women elsewhere have undergone changes with time and relocation. According to Angelo, Punjabi attitudes toward women's roles are quickly changing in North American Punjabi communities. Acceptance of, and encouragement for, an expanded role for women is now seen as reasonable by both women and men in Punjabi Sikh communities, though the possibility of such equity is not necessarily the lived experience (Steedman, 1985; Cumming and Gill, 1992; Kothandaraman, 1992; Nabar, 1992; Women of the South Asian Descent Collective, 1993; Alexander, 1996).

The research project

The choice to select this classroom as a 'critical case' is consistent with Hammersley's (1992, 1998) discussion of ethnography and Stake's (1995) view of a 'critical' case study. Because I spent such a long time observing this classroom, I noticed that many of the girls shared such silent behavior—hence, the study.

There were nine girls in Mrs. Smith's* twenty-member grade two (children aged seven) classroom in the late 1990s (11 boys, 9 girls). The specific focus on the girls allowed for a deeper frame of reference. Their behavior initially struck me as quiet. In particular, I focused oftentimes on one girl, so as to further understand the dynamics at work in more intimate ways. This girl in particular, Zara, receives much of my focus. She appeared to me to be a particularly solitary girl in that she often played alone and seemed to create opportunities to be by herself. She appeared to work slowly at her desk and often did not finish assignments in the given time. She was not one to call out answers yet was very pleased to privately show me her work on display. I wondered if she was shy or quiet in nature or if she was performing a particularly accepted and given role as a girl. If so, could it be her ethnicity in her culturally specific classroom that contributed to this silent role (that all the girls were 'like that') or was it possibly something in the classroom context itself?

The girls were all born in Canada in 1991 to Punjabi immigrants. Though their cultural roots are in the Punjab, they themselves had never visited the Punjab. They have always lived within close proximity to the school. Their parents came from India in the early 1980s. Few of their parents received a formal education in India, and most came to Canada to work on the local produce farms. The girls as well as the boys speak Punjabi at home with their families. When they started school at age five, they spoke little or no English at all. By all accounts (speech, written ability, reading ability, listening, and comprehension), they are now fluent in English and speak it spontaneously with classmates.

Their experiences with English began in their kindergarten (reception) year in 1996. At the time of my study, they had experienced two full years of English instruction and were involved in their third. They had known their classmates as constant people in their lives through both school and their communities.

Cameron (2001) says, 'language-using is an intersubjective rather than purely subjective process,' and she sees discourse analysis (and interaction analysis presumably) as a method for investigating the 'social voices' available (p. 15). My choice in developing and using a loose style of transcription came from the extensive amount of time I spent in the classroom, as well as my attempt to collect the full array of 'social voices' precisely to read like a story rather than to follow more rigorous transcription conventions used in linguistic studies.

I do not claim that my analysis of the construction of speech and silence in this language classroom can present an all-embracing picture of the girls' linguistic capabilities. The particular focus on classroom language excludes their language experiences elsewhere, such as at home or with neighbourhood friends. Nor is it possible within the constraints of such a study to respond to the enormous complexity surrounding the construction of a gendered identity that comes from society at large, from the media, and from family dynamics or individual temperament or psychology. The focus here is on describing, understanding, and analysing the construction of speech and silence and the impact of gender along with ethnicity in a language classroom—and one concerned with the girls. Because of the tremendous amount of talk that children encounter on a daily basis, and the ways in which talk may be encouraging of or antagonistic toward their participation, then an analysis of classroom talk is one important means of exploring gender in language learning experiences (Bell et al, 1993; Carspecken, 1996).

Both Stake (1995) and Flyvberg (2001) see qualitative educational research as increasingly concerned with the unique complexity of a single case and coming to understand its particular circumstances. They agree with earlier sociolinguists like Geertz (1973) and Gumperz (1982) in seeing such case studies as naturalistic, phenomenological, and largely narrative in nature. And though an intimate focus may be criticized by some as based too heavily on interpretation, the field of ESL education is and must be concerned with the intimate experiences of particular participants (Chaudron, 1988; Hammersley, 1992, 1998, 2000).

This study uses ethnographic methods because it explores what Flyvbjerg (2001) identifies as a clear 'critical case' (p. 79). By exploring one classroom, one can achieve information which 'permits logical deductions of the type' (p. 79). Flvybjerg sees such case studies as 'intense observation' that may yield more contributions to a field than large samples (p. 75).

Educational research must be primarily interested in 'critical cases', such as how someone is learning in an everyday ESL circumstance. Case study is not sampling research; Stake (1995) clarifies, 'We do not study a case primarily to understand other cases' (p. 4). For educators and researchers, there is an obligation to understand particular and specific experiences. This ethnography of one classroom is 'partly commiseration, partly celebration, but always intellectualization, a conveying, a creating of meaning' (Stake, p. 136). Gender and language education interconnect with the domains of sociology, language acquisition, feminist linguistics, and issues of pedagogy. In this sense, this 'critical case' (and at many moments a 'critical key character') is very much an interdisciplinary one in its search for the construction of speech and silence.

This Punjabi-Sikh Canadian school is one of the few independent schools operating in British Columbia which enroll children of a particular cultural and linguistic heritage. Whilst advocates for such heritage instruction have been long-standing and numerous (for example, UNESCO, 1953; Modiano, 1967; Skutnabb-Kangas and Toukomaa, 1979; Rosier and Holm, 1980; cited in Toohey, 1996a), Canada has very little reported research experience with culturally specific schools other than French or English. As such, this piece of educational case study research seeks to both identify this community and to explore and analyse the actual language experiences within it to contribute to an understanding that is helpful to educators.

Because I am using a theoretical approach of intersubjectivity, I am going to argue for my use of an 'ethnography of speaking', as articulated by Hymes (1972) and Cameron (2001). Cameron says 'ethnography of speaking' is:

> an approach to talk informed by the principles of anthropology. It focuses specifically and systematically on language-using as a cultural practice, one which is intricately related to other cultural practices and beliefs within a particular society. (p. 48)

Cameron identifies 'ethnography of speaking' as using 'situations and events' and a particular methodology of participant observation. When I, the researcher, use the role of a participant observer, I am saying that I was immersed in the everyday life of this community, as well as remaining outside, trying to understand it, trying to respond to the questions my research is seeking to answer:

1 Is there evidence of gendered use of linguistic space and of gendered speech patterns in this ESL/language classroom?
2 If so, do such patterns in the ESL classroom discourse suggest that speech and silence are being constructed?

Ethnography as research method

To answer these questions, an ethnographic method is used. There is a basic difference between qualitative and quantitative studies: the questions such research seeks to answer. Qualitative research answers more intimate, local questions (like the ones in this study), while quantitative seeks larger, generalizable results (Miles and Huberman, 1994). Qualitative data, such as the data collected in this study, is mostly verbal and so the analysis involves a process of grouping according to given categories, while quantitative data is analysed statistically. Although there is a place for quantitative research in the field of language learning and teaching, the main questions I seek to answer in this research do not lend themselves strictly to inferential statistical analysis, though a measurement of linguistic space in this classroom is provided. The quantitative data presented is considered descriptive statistics rather than empirical statistics, because the measurements communicate about the events in this classroom and are not meant to be generalisable (Weir and Roberts, 1994). It is the initial questions of enquiry that inevitably influenced what kinds of data were collected in the first place. Weir and Roberts further explain that the issue of qualitative versus quantitative methodologies is increasingly less 'contentious' (p. 162). They quote Patton (1987), saying:

> A consensus has gradually emerged that the important challenge is to match appropriate methods to evaluation questions and issues . . . and the information needs of identifiable stakeholders. (p. 162 in Weir and Roberts)

The particular use of ethnography, requires an approach that is distinct within qualitative methodology. One of its distinctive features is that the questions it seeks to answer emerge after data collection has begun rather than before (Charles, 1995). Often, pertinent questions in an ethnographic study cannot be foreseen; 'many of the most significant questions take form during the investigations' (p. 120).

Another element that sets ethnography apart from other qualitative methods, and certainly far away from quantitative ones, is that it attempts to capture a broad picture of human behavior. Ethnographic data are relatively unstructured. The collection and analysis of any qualitative data tend to be subjective and, therefore, perhaps more imprecise. This is because ethnography itself questions notions of subjectivity and objectivity and the dualistic thought this implies. Data analysis in particular is affected by, and is often criticized for, investigator bias, and conclusions often rest on evidence that may be different from what was first anticipated (Charles, 1995). But Connell et al (1982) said that critical research in education seeks to 'get close to the situations people found themselves in' (p. 29). Smith (1987) also called for an exploration of 'the actualities of what people do on a day-to-day basis under definite conditions and in definite situations' (p. 7). According to these principles, an exploration of the construction of speech and silence in this ESL classroom must use ethnographic methods and reflect on discoveries made throughout the process.

All ethnography uses, at least to some extent, participant observation. The social phenomena at work in a classroom suggest a philosophical focus on group participation with observation and analysis as the primary methods (Atkinson and Hammersley, 1998). My study proposes that the use of such qualitative methods of data collection and analysis ensure the attempt at an intersubjective understanding of Zara's ESL experiences. In this way I have been influenced by the ethnographic and/or second language research work of Cazden (1988), Carten and Stitzack (1989), Fetterman (1989), Larsen-Freeman and Long (1991), Carspecken (1996), Hey (1997), and Sheldon (1997), among many others.

Within the conceptual framework of ethnography, the problem of validity (or reliability) arises. Interpretation is obviously quite subjective. Nevertheless, the issue of validity has been addressed to some extent by way of employing certain data collection strategies. These strategies include prolonged and persistent fieldwork, verbatim accounts, low-inference descriptors, mechanically recorded data, and the more exacting role of a participant researcher. Such research strategies are used to specifically respond to the dependence on the researcher's reactions (that is, there is validity of the findings within the data itself). Though there is a general agreement within ethnography to use as many different design strategies as possible to enhance the validity of conclusions, much debate continues over the subjectivity that is so implicit in this method of research. Recent writing suggests that such concepts within the use of ethnography are still developing (Robson, 1993; Atkinson and Hammersley, 1998).

A basic and important distinction in the field of ethnography lies in the difference between the American (usually anthropological) and British (largely sociological) approaches and how ethnographies have often been polarized by such differing foci (Delamont and Atkinson, 1995). Both descriptive and analytic methods are attempted here. The role of ethnography in this study is to explore the classroom talk in an ESL classroom and in ESL girls in particular, not for the purposes of producing knowledge that is universal, but rather deliberately to study that which is more local. The high specificity and uniqueness of this study is based on a naturalistic-phenomenological philosophy that views reality as a shared social experience, thus bridging, to some extent, the more American anthropological and more British sociological views. It is, of course, assumed that the insights presented in this study will make connections with other ESL settings and with ESL teacher training in general; that is, this study is not solely for local knowledge.

Delamont and Atkinson's (1995) seminal work, *Fighting Familiarity: Essays on Education and Ethnography*, gives educational ethnographers an exhaustive critique of the past twenty years of research in classrooms: how such research divides along US/UK lines, how pseudonyms and titles are used (or not), and how the role of variables work as a lens in all classrooms. They highlight the frustrations of Becker (1971) concerning educational research; he said, 'I have talked to a couple of teams of research people who have sat around in classrooms trying to observe and it is like pulling teeth to get them to see or write anything beyond what 'everyone' knows' (p. 10 in Delamont and Atkinson). Delamont and Atkinson (1995) respond by saying that classroom ethnography is a starting-off point; that ethnography is just coming of age in its genuine attempt to make 'the familiar strange and the strange familiar' (p. 2). One person's observations of one classroom situation are highly problematic to quantitative researchers, but this subjectivity is quickly being accepted as valid and even rigorous within its own frame—that one person's account may be as valid as any other.

As a piece of qualitative, naturalistic inquiry, the use of non-interfering data collection strategy allowed for a natural display of spontaneous conversation, at times focusing on one girl in particular. Mertens (1998) articulates the importance of single participant case studies in education, saying that, though generalizability is not an immediate purpose, the understanding of particular personal experiences can contribute significantly as solid pieces of empirical research because of the information-rich informant. Zara serves the role of the main character in this story on which the theoretical ideas are hung to see if there is a 'fit'. Focusing on her at certain times allows for a narrative to be built around her.

The choice of ethnography as a research methodology is based on this study's examination of a life within a group (Geertz, 1973). Robson (1993) explains:

> [Ethnography] seeks to provide a written description of the implicit rules and traditions [within] a group. An ethnographer, through involvement with the group, tries to work out these rules. The intention is to provide a rich, or 'thick' description which interprets the experiences of people in the group from their own perspective. (p. 148)

However, the use of ethnography presents certain complexities regarding my role as researcher and my presentation of subjective data. 'The reflexive observer' of Hammersley and Atkinson (1983) is necessary in ethnography because such personal interaction disallows neutral presentation of results (p. 207). The act of interpretation therefore is more a matter of intuitive or even emotional understanding for the ethnographer than an objective description of the subjects involved (the teacher and the students) and so the data will necessarily be more narrative than chronological. The 'interplay between the personal and the emotional on the one hand, and the intellectual on the other' is the goal of ethnographic method (p. 166).

The classroom's unique set up of being part of an Indian sub-culture while surrounded by Canadian suburbia cannot but help influence discussions of identity and 'positioning'. Rampton (1995) suggested there exists 'a need for more ethnography' in order to more 'fully contextualize' the multicultural, educational experience. He saw descriptive research as under-represented in second language acquisition:

> Teachers and schools are an inextricable part of the social processes through which new ethnicities take shape. Their contribution is not easy to apprehend, it is even harder to control, and it is on (action-orientated) reflection on the school's own role that, above all, educational energies need to be expended. If standardized packages take the place of thoughtful and critical attempts to explore the school's own participation in ethnolinguistic processes, students may well be quick to detect the ersatz in language awareness modules on multilingualism, and respond to them accordingly. (p. 335)

Ethnographic research is guided by a focus to understand the culture both from an 'emic' (insider) and 'etic' (outsider) perspective (Mertens, 1998, p. 165). Atkinson and Hammersley (1998) note a tension in ethnographic research concerning objectivity or the ability to produce scientific knowledge that is universally valid. However, an intensive and detailed study of one classroom and one participant within it allows for an opportunity to understand the way gender may be constructed in this particular instance.

Ethnography is also emerging as an important strategy in the search for the validation of particular language learning experiences, such as ESL. Hymes's (1972) 'ethnography of speaking' is concerned with language use over the traditional linguistics concern with language structure. Coulthard (1985) also devoted much of his early research to defining the speech community and how speech styles emerge from within such communities. As such, Coulthard believes that the aim of an 'ethnography of speaking' is perhaps 'an exhaustive list of the speech acts and speech events of a particular speech community' (p.

42). Both Hymes and Coulthard go on to identify certain elements of conversation (including backchannel support, turn-taking, tag questions) though they do not specifically address gender in the performance of spoken interaction. And so, though ethnography is slow work, an ethnographic focus can illuminate issues in the classroom and can reveal the complexities of social problems beyond more conventional quantitative research.

Building an ethnographic relationship

I focus here on the experiences of one second grade ESL classroom (seven year olds), over forty hours of classroom observation. I collected this data on a weekly basis beginning in September and concluding in June of the school year. The amount of data spanning ten full months in the life of this classroom strengthens the validity of this study. (Stake, 1995, identified most case studies as spanning only a few weeks.)

The entire class was observed weekly. I took continuous field notes of my observations and videotaped the children as they went about their activities (sometimes with the help of a video technician and sometimes on my own). I focused my observations on the classroom dynamics and activities, seen exclusively in the video data and the complete transcriptions of the videos. Again, the gesture to appear focused on the entire classroom was done to protect Zara's anonymity and to ensure a non-disruptive position in the classroom. Weir and Roberts (1994) explore such 'unobtrusiveness' in their discussion on 'observer effect' (p. 173). They suggested that the researcher/observer be as 'unobtrusive as possible' as well as frequent, 'making a sufficient number of observations' (p. 174).

Each morning visit lasted two hours on average (some visits being one and a half hours, other visits being three hours). I was aware of my position as observer, as adult, as researcher, and also of my physical proximity to the group. I intentionally varied arrangements to provide opportunity for various social dynamics. I sometimes joined in for play time and I sometimes sat at a back desk. The physical arrangement of the desks changed once during my time in the classroom. Otherwise, my movement through the desk groupings, the free play activities, and the circle time arrangement provided ample shifts in context.

During my observations, I systematically noted where all the children in the classroom were sitting and any activities that occurred to help with the transcriptions. I took note of such physical arrangements because of Mahony's (1985) discovery that 'girls are often found in the role of spectator; they sit and watch boys' activities' (p. 26). In classroom discussions, girls take up less physical space than boys, though my focus settled exclusively on the classroom talk. Because the teacher's talk predominates, her speech figures prominently in the transcripts.

The classroom talk is transcribed as I heard it and recorded it over the course of the school year. In my attempt to manage the enormous amount of data, it is transcribed and written like a drama script, as previously explained. My decision to present the data in this form was influenced by Cameron's (2001) view of discourse analysis as able to adjust to the goals of the particular study. She says that various styles can be used to match the various research projects.

After reviewing transcription conventions from Flanders (1990), Ochs (1996), Tannen (1989), and Coates (1993, 1996), I became convinced that the location of this research in an educational tradition was not to be aligned with a linguistic or critical discourse analysis which would use a different kind of attention to the transcription process and to the presentation of the classroom talk in these transcripts. As such, the transcripts and quotations of the transcripts are deliberately and conscientiously presented as a drama script and more in keeping with Chaudron's (1988) interaction analysis used in other ESL classroom research. My adaptation from various methods is in keeping with an 'ethnography of speaking' approach, as well as an intersubjective view of 'social voices' (Cameron, 2001). Also, because one girl often serves as the story's main character, this focus lends itself to a script-style of transcription.

This language classroom

In examining the experiences of these girls, it was important to consider the surrounding evidence of gender roles in the classroom and in the ethos of the school. The principal was male and so were the temple leaders who oversaw the morning worship before classes began each day. The hallways of the school were filled with portraits of the ten gurus of Sikhism, all male.

Within the classroom itself, there were marginally more boys than girls. The classroom was large and brightly decorated. The room was filled with books. Various classroom projects were posted on the many bulletin boards. Also, building block toys and a playhouse area were in the room.

Unlike children in Canadian public/state schools, the children in this school wore a school uniform (white shirt, black sweater, dark pants), though each with a particular variation--perhaps the school sweater not worn or an extra or different coloured sweater added. Apart from physical differences such as height, weight or hairstyle, these students shared a particular physical appearance. These details initially framed my observations though I eventually ceased to notice them.

Each day began with students arriving, going to class, greeting their teacher, and finding their scarves for worship. Such scarves were kept in their desks all year long. Students quickly put on their scarves, hung up any coats or knapsacks in the coat check area of their room, and lined up for worship, which began at 8:40 each morning and consisted of a thirty-minute reading in Punjabi of a sacred text. Together, the children and community shared the routines of their religious and linguistic heritage.

After the service, the students returned to their classroom for story time, calendar and weather discussion, basic language arts activities, free play, mathematics, and reading (essentially in that order). These lessons were conducted completely in English. Lunch was often served in the dining hall. Mrs. Smith and her class sometimes ate together, enjoying prepared cultural foods familiar to them. Other classes occasionally joined them, depending on the particular schedules of varying grades.

Following lunch and outside playtime, the students returned to their classroom for Sikh and Punjabi studies conducted by the community elders. Throughout the school day, the students' cultural identity and cultural sense of belonging were being reinforced by both male and female authority figures in and around the school community. The school principal, secretary, substitute teacher, and bus driver were Punjabi Sikhs and adhered to the Khalsa codes regarding dress. Because of this culturally specific environment of relative cultural unity, the language-learning experiences were unique within a context where fellow students were coming from similar starting points in contrast to mainstream schools where there is linguistic and cultural diversity.

Focusing the project

With my intersubjective theoretical approach, I could not describe the girls as isolated individuals, or as 'objects' of research. My understanding of them was deeply embedded in my own relationship with them and embedded in their own relationships within the classroom. Early in the research, Zara was no more significant than any of the other children, boys included. As previously mentioned, the extensive amount of observation time propelled me to see that a focus on one girl would allow for an intersubjective understanding of the construction of speech and silence. Because of the aim to explore the construction of speech and silence in female language students, it appeared most feasible and beneficial to focus the observations around a specific girl as a main character. What also became clear was that, in the light of the low percentage of female speech in this classroom, it made little difference which girl was selected as a focus character. The silence that became a frustrating element to document eventually appeared as something that would have been encountered with any other girl in this classroom: that is, all the girls were relatively quiet. The few times a girl spoke in classroom discussions, it was more often than not the same girl. But, even if the more talkative girl had been the focus character, she could only have been more talkative to a point.

Segments of literacy lesson times were isolated and analysed in a stratified random sample so that similar lessons of full group discussions were selected. Monthly samples were chosen as samples to scan the experiences throughout the school year. As such, ten segments were pulled from the transcripts and the words of teacher-talk/student-talk were counted and measured for percentages of linguistic space. Within student-talk, both boy-talk and girl-talk were then measured by counting actual words to focus on the amount of linguistic participation of the girls in these classroom moments. Following from such analysis, the type of 'speech acts' was documented to gain a sense of linguistic context (Searle, 1969). The ten segments were deliberately screened for similar-type classroom moments so that all are teacher-led lessons or 'group' discussions; none are small group or collaborative discussions as such.

During the analysis and writing stage, the transcriptions were organised around two broad themes: what the teacher says and what the girls say in classroom conversations, specifically looking for evidence of female speech strategies. Silence was a consistent feature of linguistic behavior in all the girls, though such a feature appeared too elusive to document. And so I eventually measured, by way of word-count, the amount of linguistic space used by the teacher, the boys, the girls, and Zara as a focus character during classroom lessons.

A profile on Zara's classroom experiences was initially the main layer of analysis. It was only after reflection on my interview with the teacher that I came to see the teacher's presence in Zara's experience as possibly helpful in understanding Zara's very quiet year. Organizing the data helped me focus on a main theme: that gender may be a significant predictor of classroom speech and silence.

Because the girls ultimately spoke so rarely, these sections of the data were obvious and any researcher would have found the same ones: when they talked during lesson time, I pulled these moments to use for analysis. In qualitative research, ethnography, as both a form of observation and of analysis, uniquely allows for classroom 'stories' to be told. That I am present in the observation as a participant observer, explicitly aware of my own subjectivity, follows from current intersubjective beliefs about ethnography and self-reflection in research. In attempting to understand the speech and the silence in language classrooms, this study focuses on a particular classroom. Such an intimate focus is in keeping with my theoretical approach of intersubjectivity.

Ultimately, ethnography is story-telling. Though others might have told a different story, what exists here is one legitimate telling of this ESL classroom. For this study, the variable of gender as well as a marginalized Punjabi identity impact upon the story as significant and crucial details in the construction of classroom participation based on gender.

These girls lived in a unique classroom, different than ESL girls attending public, mainstream schools. Their different classroom experiences are related to their position within a particular ethnic community where all their classmates shared a cultural heritage. In this regard, they had much in common. The theory of intersubjectivity attempts to ground the issue of individual participation within social settings and, in this case, its relationship to speech and silence.

*All names have been changed to protect confidentiality.

5

Teacher Talk and Linguistic Space

The teacher talk which surrounds the students in their language classroom is an integral part of their classroom experience and, therefore, a central element in their learning of English. The methods used by the teacher may suggest an objectified perception of the students with no mirrored-self of intersubjectivity. Also, the fact that Mrs. Smith's students are in a language classroom to learn to speak English problematizes the lack of speech production, particularly on the part of the girls in this context, making their silence ironic. If they are in a language learning classroom, why are they rarely speaking?

Mrs. Smith expressed her views about teaching, ethnicity, and gender in an hour-long interview with me at the end of the school year. She also revealed her views in her conversations with her students, as evidenced in teacher-led classroom discussions. I seek here to track the particular currents at work in this classroom and the meanings which inform and drive the learning climate.

Mrs. Smith did not have any specific preparation in her teacher training for teaching ESL, though she said that she saw her role as uniquely involved with the language learning for this group of children, supported by a wide range of institutional and curricular goals, particularly concerning phonics.

Linguistic space

As reviewed in Chapter 3, teacher talk is a major part of any classroom (Clarricoates, 1978; Spender, 1980a; Stanworth, 1981; Mahony, 1985; Thompson, 1989; Corson, 1993; Thornborrow, 2002). A teacher-dominated lesson is typical (see Flanders, 1970). However, the overwhelming amount of teacher talk in Mrs. Smith's language classroom is curious because of what is thought to occur in language classrooms. In each of the ten segments of teacher-led classroom time used for measurement of linguistic space, Mrs. Smith uses 89.4% of the linguistic space. Girls speak for roughly 2%. This lack of linguistic space for students supports Flanders early 'two-thirds' of classroom talk is teacher talk. The findings also relate to the greater use of linguistic space used by boys, found in Soskin and John, 1963; Stubbs, 1976; Mahony, 1985; Graddol and Swann, 1989.

Many of the full-class discussions or lessons in this language classroom regularly involve interactions of Mrs. Smith and her male students, with the girls appearing most often as observers of the classroom talk. An over-concern for the contributions of boys is discussed in the work of Stanworth (1981), Mahony (1985), and Swann and Stubbs (1992) and others discussed in Chapter 3. What is evident in this classroom is a 9:1 (boys:girls) ratio of the use of the linguistic space. This consistent discrepancy in the amount of talk used by boys over girls over ten months, the full school year, may alert ESL teachers to gender as a factor in language production in ESL classrooms. Perhaps the initiation/response/follow up method is not as effective a method for girls in mixed classes.

It is clear in the data that the conversations in this classroom are dominated primarily by Mrs. Smith and, secondarily, by the boys. In fact, in the first ten minutes of the data, a girl speaks only four times to the twenty-two contributions made by boys in the class. This imbalance is consistent throughout the ten months of observation. The disproportion of time used by the girls does not shift as the year progresses; instead, the lack of linguistic space remains a constant for both the girls and the boys in this classroom.

In the analysis of the amount of talk used by all of the participants in the room (the teacher, the boys, the girls) ten segments of full-class lesson time, each of five minutes, were used. A sample of such lessons is provided here:

Mrs. Smith: Was it rainy and cloudy? Sort of a mix-max. So a little bit of sun, little bit of clouds, tiny little bit of rain, just a little dot. Just a little dotsy part? And it was 18. 18. Just a little bit of rain, because most of the day it was nice, it wasn't pouring at all. Okay. Today it's 19 and what have we got?

Students: Rain, rain.

Mrs. Smith:	(drawing drops of rain on calendar) Lots of rain, lots of rain. ...You can hear it. It sounds like that, doesn't it? 19. 19. Okay? ...Now, let's . . . (She moves over to the chair and the class follows and sits on the carpet. She ties up a boy's shoe for him.)
Girl:	(says something to Ally off-camera. Ally responds and girl shakes her head.) It's a secret.
Mrs. Smith:	... Okay, yesterday we read... or the day before, two probably. The story of Little Red Riding Hood. AND... we had someone who was good and who was a ...?
Class:	Little Red Riding Hood.
Mrs. Smith:	Little Red Riding Hood. And we had someone who was *bad*. Who was that?
Class:	Wolf. Big wolf...
Mrs. Smith:	The big wolf. And we had someone else who was good...?
Class:	Grandma.
Mrs. Smith:	Hunter. The hunter. In that story, we had THREE of the good guys, but ONE of the bad guy. Alright. What about the story of the Three Little Pigs? Who were the good guys?
Class:	Three little pigs.
Mrs. Smith:	The three pigs. Who was the bad guy?
Class:	The wolf.
Mrs. Smith:	The wolf. The wolf. Right. In that story. Okay. In the story 'Cinderella'... Cinderella. Some of you know the story 'Cinderella.' Who were the good guys?
Boy 1:	The prince.
Mrs. Smith:	The prince.
Boy 2:	And Cinderella.
	Mrs. Smith: And Cinderella. Who were the bad guys?
Students:	Stepmother, step-sisters.
Mrs. Smith:	... and the three sisters. Right. So every story is different, but some of the fairy-tale type stories have something that's good and something that's bad. Someone who's good and someone who's bad. Because that's what makes the story interesting. Today we had all those bi, oh, those good kids but there was someone who was doing something bad. The magic that changed them. It wasn't really bad. It wasn't really gross like

	the other story, but it was something bad, and that's what makes the story interesting. So, today in your journal, you're going to write a story, you're going to pick someone who's good and someone or something or some...how, that's BAD. And you're going to tell the story. So you can start 'Once upon a time, there was a ...', or you can start 'One day a...' and you can tell me the story. But you have to think, now, who's going to be in my story? Am I going to put people in my story? Am I going to put animals in my story?
Students:	Yeah.
Mrs. Smith:	Is it going to be ALL animals? Or all people?
Class:	No.
Mrs. Smith:	Alright. What's going to happen? Is it going to be a trip? Is it going to be a chase? Is it going to be a race?
Boys:	Ha ha. Race. Race.
Mrs. Smith:	Mmm. What's going to happen?
Student:	Race.
Mrs. Smith:	The last question is, 'Who's going to win?'
Students:	The good guys!
Mrs. Smith:	Who's gonna win?
Students:	Good guys. Good guys.

Classroom Visit #9

Such lessons occurred each morning of observation as part of the literacy or language hour. This particular segment seems an interesting piece to introduce the classroom energy (Short and Carrington, 1989). The sample not only reveals some binary stereotypes surrounding male and female characters (that is, the prince is good, the stepsisters are bad, that good Cinderella is rescued) or that the notions of 'good' and 'bad' seem to be traditional views that the teacher elicits from her students without much indication of prompting, but also that the teacher does most of the talking.

Ten similar types of teacher-led classroom moments were isolated and then analysed by counting the words produced by the teacher, the boys, the girls, and then Zara as a key silent character. Also examined was the average length of utterances used by boys and girls, as well as the number of times each gender group attempted to contribute. A synopsis of the linguistic breakdown is seen on the following two charts displaying the results. The first chart includes the teacher in the analysis, whereas the second chart isolates the students' use of linguistic space. In this way, the gender differences are clearer in the second chart:

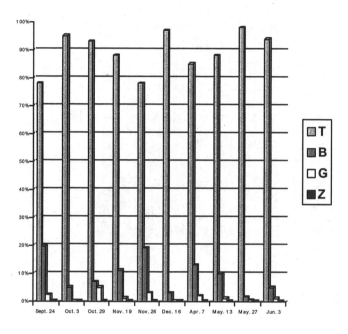

Chart 5.1   Linguistic Space of the Classroom

T: Teacher

B: Boys

G: Girls

Z: Zara

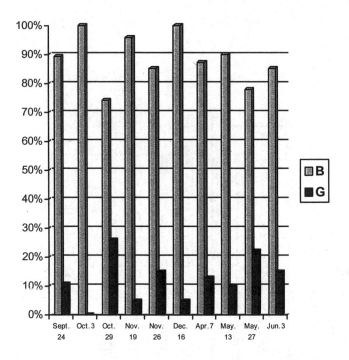

Chart 5.2   The Gendered Linguistic Space

B: Boys

G: Girls

As evidenced in the charts, the use of linguistic space is not divided equally between the boys and girls. Because each of the lessons were similar concerning the type of interaction, that is, all were similar full-class discussions, it becomes apparent that the teacher dominates the literacy time. On average, the teacher speaks for 89.4% of the time (ranging from 78% to 97%). Her students, on average, use 10.5% of the remaining talk (ranging from 2% to 22%). Of this, boys speak for most of the time (88.3%). Girls speak for 11.7% of the linguistic space left over to the students. In other words, girls speak only 1.29% of the total discussion time with the teacher (ranging from 0% to only 3% at the most).

Of the students' speech events, 9.5 words on average are spoken at one time, and only the boys have such a length of duration. Girls only reach an average of a 5.5 word response, though one girl says a full ten words at one time. As such, the linguistic production on the part of all the children is minimal but the girls in particular are almost non-existent in the classroom discussions.

Zara is completely silent. In the light of the silence of other girls in the room, it appears that most of the nine girls are similarly quiet. The minimal amount of linguistic space used by students contrasts sharply with a similar analysis of linguistic space I did on their classroom the previous grade one year. The linguistic space in that classroom in similar-style lessons breakdown, on average, as follows:

Teacher:	82%
Students:	18%
Boys:	12%
Girls:	6%

As such, with a different teacher in the grade one sample, the teacher:student ratio of the amount of talk is 4 to 1 compared to the 9 to 1 ratio in Mrs. Smith's room with the same group of children. Perhaps, if the silence of these girls was something ethnically required or promoted, then a similar amount of linguistic space would exist in both classrooms. But it does not. What may be happening then, is that the particular teaching practices construct the learning differently (even with the same learners) in any given classroom.

Speech acts

In light of these findings, it may be reasonable to suggest that it is the teacher who may be 'gendering' the classroom talk by privileging the boys over the girls in some way. It is helpful, therefore, to explore the type of language being used. I counted each utterance used by each participant and then organized these utterances into classifications of what Searle (1969) and Cameron (2001) called 'speech acts.' The categories in the breakdown of language used in this classroom come from my extensive observations of the classroom over the ten months. In this, I am following an ethnography of speaking model to organize the types of speech acts relevant to this particular classroom setting (that is, I have used some of my own categories that seem best able to match with the classroom discussions).

Table 5.1 Teacher Speech Acts

Speech act	To the class	To a boy	To a girl	Total
Question	67	11	1	79
Repetition of a student's comment	10	44	5	59
Explanation	32	1	0	33
Negative response to a question	7	20	4	31
Instruction/guidance	28	0	0	28
Positive response	5	14	5	24
Direct order	1	10	2	13
Ignoring student's comment	0	10	2	12
Criticism	0	8	2	10
Praise/reinforcement	1	3	0	4
General comment	3	0	0	3
Story-telling	2	0	0	2

Table 5.2 Student Speech Acts

Speech act	Group	Boys	Girls	Total
Response to a question	15	57	8	80
Uninitiated comment	0	21	3	24
Question to teacher	0	1	1	2
Story-telling	0	1	0	1

The most frequently used speech act by Mrs. Smith was questioning (79 occurrences). She generally directed her questions to the class as a whole (67 times), then to the boys (11 times), and only once directly to a girl. She often repeated a student's comment as recognition of their contribution (a total of 59 times). This was most often done in response to a boy's comment (44 times) while only a few times to a girl (5 times), almost a 9:1 ratio.

The teacher question-response-evaluation pattern confirms other research describing classroom speech acts. In these classroom discussions the conversation was generally between Mrs. Smith and the boys in her class: she usually asked questions (79 occurrences) and these were usually answered by boys (57 responses by boys to a question).

Mrs. Smith also used explanation and instruction in her talk, followed closely by negative or positive comments (negative responses: 31; positive: 24). Of her responses, most were directed to boys (24 times) over girls (only 9 times) or 2.5:1. Negative comments were directed to boys more often than to girls (20:4 or 5:1) as were positive comments (14:5 or almost 3:1). Mrs. Smith offered praise four times: once to the whole class and three times to a boy. There was no speech act of praise given to a girl. This discrepancy of attention is similar to what Mahony (1985) found in her study.

The students' speech acts were usually responses to Mrs. Smith's questions—the teacher initiation/response/follow-up strategy. However, with this method the boys were the usual and consistent responders. The boys called out answers (21 such acts in boys to only 3 in girls, 7:1). Only two questions originated with the students themselves—one from a boy and one from a girl. There was one speech act of a student sharing information and this was a boy's.

The table shows the results of the kinds of speech acts that account for the types of things said and further illuminates the linguistic environment in this language classroom. Girls rarely speak. The few times a girl does speak, she offers short phrasal comments, such as: 'He planted apple-seeds' or 'They call them apple-seeds' (Classroom Visit #2) while the boys' responses were often more substantial in length, such as: '. . . and she climbed up all the tree, then she didn't say help, then she couldn't help the fire truck came then she came down' (Classroom Visit #3). Boys not only spoke more often, they also said more.

Such speech patterns are pervasive throughout the data, from the first classroom visit through to the end of the ten months of observation in this class. It is only in the smaller activity groups that one can get a sense of the girls' speech at all. The girls' speech production is primarily located in one-to-one peer interactions and rarely do these one-to-one conversations involve the teacher. There may be a reason for the lack of a relationship between the girls and their teacher. When the teacher was asked in the interview to comment on the classroom and then the girls in particular, it appeared she may not hold strong views.

Much of what the teacher said suggested that her view of her students' ethnic identity is somewhat limited regarding immigration and the complex reality of the immigrant experience. She says, 'They have to live here because they know it's better,' perhaps implying that Canada provides the Punjabi immigrants with a 'better' life from one possibly experienced in India. But she also adds the instruction to 'them' that they need to 'obey rules' (implying that 'they' do not obey rules):

Allyson: Do you think they see themselves as Canadians or...?

Mrs. Smith: I'm not sure because it's hard to tell at this age. Uhm, as people they take the best of everything which is what we do and so I don't know how that really works, for some, they still hold onto India. They have to live here because they know it's better but I think they still hold on tightly without adapting a little bit so that they can enjoy it. And I'm not saying give up that, I'm saying adapt *with* that. Don't lose that! Keep your traditions, keep your celebrations, keep your history and whatever, *but* add on some of the nice things, and obey rules and things that are made for the safety of all.

Further evidence of the teacher's views of ethnicity follow, particularly her claim that future employers (presumably 'white' Canadians) may not be satisfied with Punjabi employees because they are not 'smart':

Mrs. Smith: Language arts is the *main thing* that *has* to be taught. And I will give up other things to get that done. They have to be able to read and write English in order to get jobs, in order to survive in the future. It is a life skill they must have if they're going to live in Canada. So that is my educational priority, they have to speak it, they have to read it, they have to write it. And I'm forever telling them you know, when you say that it makes you look stupid when you're not. You have to say it properly you have to say it, you know. And with enough confidence that people will believe you. Because your employer will say, 'yeah right! I want him!' And I say, you're just as smart as everybody else, you have as much chance but you have to think and say things that are showing that that smart and that's something this whole group is really bad at, as a group. They will say, like I will say, 'okay, we're going swimming, you need a bathing suit and a towel and a bathing suit and we're going to the pool and we're going to have waves.' Three kids will put up their hand and say, 'where are we going Mrs. Smith?' That's not smart.

Mrs. Smith's statement, 'I'm forever telling them you know, when you say that it makes you look stupid when you're not' may suggest that she understands social racism and seeks to make her students aware of what they may face in future situations—situations not as homogeneous as their classroom. She may also hold to an assimilationist view that the Punjabi language is a negative element, a feature that needs to be masked or hidden away from mainstream 'Canadian' culture so that an 'employer' (a white Canadian, perhaps) would not view these Punjabi children as 'stupid' if overheard speaking Punjabi or speaking English incorrectly. Perhaps Mrs. Smith says this because she acknowledges that society views the Punjabis as marginalized, less important, less significant, less valuable than other 'Canadians'. She says, 'That's something this whole group is really bad at, as a group.' She goes on to say that 'they' don't listen well or remember things; ultimately, she says, 'that's not smart.' Perhaps Mrs. Smith is trying to help her Punjabi students be more accepted.

The teacher discusses the students as a marked group, not like 'regular kids' who do 'regular activities'. In this way, she appears to use a double standard in her view of her ESL students:

Allyson: What are the advantages that you see in them for having their child [in this school]?

Mrs. Smith: For having their culture, for having their reading, writing Punjabi, for learning their music, for learning their stories, for having their history, those are all advantages for sure of being here. For being in proximity with their own adults, their own grandparents and stuff, for having them learn. Like when we were free to run through the dining hall and stuff, for eating their own food, for being their own community. And also because of the teachers having excursions out to join up with the other things that are happening with regular kids, regular activities.

These words reveal that, when asked about the advantages of having a culturally specific school, the teacher lists surface elements of 'their' community: music, stories, history, food. She does not reveal possible beliefs about the advantages of bilingualism or an 'ethnic' identity. Instead, the teacher sees Punjabiness as something that needs to be managed or assimilated.

She sees herself in the role of cultural informant of things 'Canadian', which suggests a view toward the Punjabis that 'they' need to be informed about Canadian culture.   She says, 'I do a lot of the songs that are typical of Canadians.'   However, I heard no recognizable songs, apart from the national anthem, in the classroom throughout the entire ten months.   ('Come, come, come to the carpet' is not a piece of 'Canadian culture'.)   This chant was heard in each of the transcriptions.   That the teacher saw herself as a cultural informant and, at times, performed a deliberate role in this regard reflects on her attitudes about Punjabiness as a deficit and assimilation into English Canadian nation-building as desirable.   She sees 'Punjabi' and 'Canadian' as separate identities and not intersubjective or mixed.

Mrs. Smith: Uhm, my biggest priority is to make sure that they get what they need.   So that if they ever have to transfer or if they have to *live*—period-- they're not at a disadvantage in any way from any other child who would be given a learning opportunity or given whatever they need.   So that's one of the priorities.   Another priority would be to make sure they have enough Canadiana, to be able to join in when they want to join in, to appreciate their new country, to learn how to fit into their new country and obey the laws and that there are some things you can and can't do and that there's lots of wonderful things you can enjoy and experience.   But don't lose your culture and your own identity, your own heritage.

The comment, 'If they have to live – period - they're not at a disadvantage in any way from any other child' further communicates her view of Punjabiness as 'a disadvantage', not preparing them 'to live - period'.   In this she reveals the attitude towards minority ethnicities, as described in Cummins and Danesi (1990) as 'a pathological condition to be overcome' (p. 9).   What is also curious here is Mrs. Smith's choice of the word 'new', that these children need enough 'Canadiana to be able to join in' their 'new country'.   But all of these students are Canadian, born and raised in British Columbia, and a part of a multicultural community that on one level recognizes them in a multicultural Canada while at another sees them as foreign and 'new'.   She also says, 'But don't lose your culture and your own identity, your own heritage.'   In this, perhaps she is revealing the complexity at work in ESL classrooms everywhere.

In this next excerpt, Mrs. Smith reveals her view of Punjabi students as disadvantaged and of herself as a cultural guide:

Allyson: Are there extra activities you do with this classroom?

Mrs. Smith: It has impacted in that we have not been able to do the field-trips to the other schools, have other schools here, go out to visit as much and I think that is a very important part of the program because these children cannot be isolated from Canadiana, from speech, from activities, uhm, I don't want them to think they're different, I want to them to think they're kids, that they can share, that they can play in the neighbourhood, that they can transfer things back and forth, that it's universal. Soccer is universal, it doesn't have to be played by black kids or white kids, it just has to be played with a ball on a space. So I'm trying to change attitudes.

Allyson: Do you think that they see themselves as different?

Mrs. Smith: Uhm, if they're isolated they could. These children do not. And I'm sure they think I'm East Indian too, like they do not differentiate me from them either because of the loyalty that we have for each other, I think. But I think if we were isolated from each other, they could. Like I do a lot of the songs that are typical of Canadian ... they hear them other places, I do skipping rhymes that are typically Canadian ... and they hear them other places.

Again, Mrs. Smith expresses a somewhat limited understanding of the Punjabi Sikh experience though she recognizes a form of equality between groups ('soccer is universal'). She takes little account of the fact that the community is already engaged in neighbourhood activities; she seems unaware of the possibility that the children may already have meaningful friendships with 'Canadian' children outside of the classroom walls. She gives little sense of being aware of their TV viewing or participation on sports teams. She says, 'I'm trying to change attitudes,' but what attitudes is she trying to change? And what is she trying to change them into? At best, she is unaware of a complex, complete life outside of what she sees. She says, 'I'm sure they think I'm East Indian, too,' but how could this be, especially when she sees herself as the one Canadian in their lives, their informant of all things Canadian?

Mrs. Smith also expresses strong opinions about the girls, Zara in particular, explicitly saying that Zara's family is 'dysfunctional', that Zara is not encouraged or guided or led or supported by them. This view suggests that Mrs. Smith feels all-knowing about the life of Zara. Mrs. Smith highlights Zara's new earrings and dress, while at the same time she does not recognize that such gifts were most likely from her 'dysfunctional' family. Why does Mrs. Smith see herself as such a missionary to Zara, that Zara is 'rock bottom', and needing saving? Yet the teacher shows knowledge, caring, understanding of Zara's background and does appear to encourage her and praise her. The following transcription reveals these competing views:

Allyson: Tell me about Zara.

Mrs. Smith: Zara, basically I would tell you I would like to take her home and basically spend some time and whatever spoiling her and loving her and whatever. She has a family that's dysfunctional. Mother is working hard but Zara has excuses why she can't do this that and the other. She is not encouraged, she is not guided, she is not led and supported. So therefore she hasn't learned responsibility, she hasn't learned how to get things put in a... I don't know how you put it. Now, I told you she got new earrings, wore a dress, I praised her and spoiled her for this because it shows a feminine thing which she wasn't allowed to have. She has a brother who's a behavior problem, caused a lot of problems for the school, running with some other boys who were a bad influence and he had to be on discipline all day every day. And she's running that with no sort of catch up—no praise for her to be different, no encouragement for her to be different—to be more academic, to be better, and whatever. So I have mainly encouraged her to be a little girl, encouraged her to be responsible, encouraged her to show pride in what she does, not to just drag around and let everything happen. Academically, extremely low when she came, very rock bottom when she came--no reading, no understanding. She has no background in that kind of stuff, I think, I'm sure, Now if she does it's very limited. Uhm, I've done a lot of extra thing in saying you know, look you can't do that, that is not the way you're going to do it, you're a very smart girl. All of a sudden, in math, she has gone almost to the top. She does not pick up a concept easily but once she gets it—she gets it. In adding and subtracting for a while she was *the* top student, no mistakes. So that encouraged her to try a little bit more in reading. And although she is low because she can't follow directions and she can't choose words and she doesn't have the academic background to know what it means and what things are she has picked up like 2000 per cent since the beginning of the year. And she is beginning to get it. The problem with that is that it's late now, it should have happened earlier, but at least it did happen. And if she is encouraged next she may just run with it and she may be able to overcome the family things she has that are still holding her back.

Mrs. Smith seems to want to make clear to me that she knows much, including the past experiences of Zara. She knows much about Zara's family but, also of significance, is the definition she offers of 'feminine', saying that the new earrings and dress needed Mrs. Smith's encouragement. She says, 'it shows a feminine thing which [Zara] wasn't allowed to have.' If she was not allowed these things, then how did she get them? And why does the teacher hold these out as symbols of being female or as signals of being cared for as a girl? She also communicates that 'to be a little girl' means to be 'responsible.' My request was simply, 'Tell me about Zara.' It was Mrs. Smith herself who wished to communicate that gender was contributing to Zara's weaknesses as a student: she was not being a very 'good girl'. The conversation continued:

Allyson: What about her friends?
Mrs. Smith: Uhm—Zara sticks with the kids but they don't really like her because of some of her deviant behavior.
Allyson: Like what?
Mrs. Smith: Annoying little things that she does, picky, picky, picky. One thing she does is she gets right your face and she just yells at you and I'm *sure* that's a family thing. That's probably what her brother does, her mum does, her dad does and I'm sure that's how you do it. So she'll get right in your face really close and she'll just yell at you, even if you're a friend of hers. So it's really ... I've talked to her about that. Do you want to be

treated like that? And I've done it to her and she hates it. But I thought, 'you've got to see how it feels from the other side'... so that you know but I monitor that behavior very carefully because I do not want it to stick. Right now she's with NP, um, SN, and JE. Okay she's sitting with them in that group. But tomorrow she could be kicked out of the group and gone because of her annoying naggy little whatevers. Okay?

Mrs. Smith's claim, 'I'm sure that's a family thing,' is perhaps evidence that she sees Zara as a problem which results from her life in a dysfunctional family, one that is unable to adequately support her. Is this why Mrs. Smith says in this next excerpt that it is her role to 'really love her' and 'to give her a different lifestyle'?:

Allyson: What about her personality?
Mrs. Smith: Personally she's very hard to get along with because of this blast and, or whatever; she has a lot of behavior of her brothers which she doesn't need to have but it's not discouraged at home. So that's why I would like to take her home, really love her, and give her a different lifestyle and I'm sure she'd be a totally different kid. You know, in a year you'd see totally different things because it's not there built in for her. And the mom says, you know, 'well I'm a single mum' and I say, 'well I was too.' You know that not an excuse, you have to work harder, 'well I work all day, all night.' So she doesn't get her books back because she was at uncle's last night and she was up late and she couldn't find them. And she doesn't get her homework back because she couldn't do it because they dragged her here and dragged her there; I mean there's a lot of things in her lifestyle that do not allow her to gain academic progress. And that's sad. It's sad.

In these lengthy comments, perhaps the language teacher sees the young girl as an aggressive and annoying child who needs the love and attention of an adult (one like herself) who could train her in feminine ways. Mrs. Smith expresses the inadequacies of the mother in particular as the reason for Zara's improper conduct. In the collected video data, there is no evidence of the behavior the teacher describes, the kind of 'in your face' yelling that she isolates as a problem in Zara's demeanor. The teacher says Zara needs training to become more appropriately female, 'a little girl'. She expresses Zara's failure in this regard and supports the earlier claim emerging from other feminist research that such views of femaleness (as quiet, reserved, and responsible) cross ethnic lines (Brah and Minhas, 1985; Paechter, 1998).

The teacher displays a gender stereotype toward her ESL students. Is this exaggerated by their Punjabiness? It seems safe to say that Zara may be constructed as a problem or at least as a special case needing correction. The characters in Zara's world, such as her mother, her brother, her father, are viewed as problems. Zara's life is defined as inadequate in permitting her or preparing her to function as a learner. The teacher wants to correct her, wants to take her home, and wants to provide her with proper guidance. Perhaps such an attitude is a common view of some teachers: to serve as social workers. Perhaps the teacher sees Zara's entire world is flawed and not valuable—or perhaps her views are more motherly and protective. But Mrs. Smith, in either option, provides some affirmation regarding Zara's potential, saying that she could be taught through her problems and be made better, made more 'female' and more 'Canadian'.

Mrs. Smith sees the other girls as rejecting Zara for good reason. Zara's personality is viewed as a negative thing; she is 'hard to get along with', while no mention is made of the flaws in the other girls as to why relationships might be strained, if in fact they are. The teacher's belief that one needs to be a 'good girl' seems to produce the effect it seeks because Zara does demonstrate quiet behavior (Gal, 1991; Goldberger, 1997). Mrs. Smith's comments about Zara suggest a different reality from that seen in the research videotapes. Zara is not seen to 'yell' in someone's face and no video data revealed such behavior. Perhaps, the teacher's views come from elsewhere and are fed largely by a myth of female behavior. It is possible that Zara might have displayed this yelling, aggressive behavior when I was not present or when the video camera was not playing (Weir and Roberts's 'observer effect', 1994). Zara might have sensed I was studying her and, as a result, her behavior might have been more guarded when I was present. However, considering the length of time (10 months) and the hour and a half weekly visits, it seems unlikely that Zara would have been able to sustain one kind of behavior when I was there and a completely different set of behaviors at other times. In the remotest possibility that this was so, one might expect that the teacher herself might have noticed a sudden shift in protocol when I was present but none was mentioned.

Mrs. Smith's classroom speech

Mrs. Smith reveals her attitudes towards gender and/or ethnicity in classroom talk with all her students. In the following excerpts, examples of many such in the transcripts, it is clear that the boys are interacting with Mrs. Smith with ease and that she sees herself as a the source of all things Canadian. She does not seem to be as responsive to the girls in her classroom as she is to the boys, a pattern also seen in the work of Spender and Sarah (1980), Stanworth (1981), Mahony (1985), Lakoff (1995), and Paechter (1998). Mrs. Smith constructs herself as the only true Canadian in the room; and she often ignores the girls or interacts with them by correcting them or dismissing the contributions they do make. It is through such practices that the silence is understood and these methods may help explain why the girls remain so quiet.

The teacher as a 'true Canadian'

This excerpt of classroom talk focuses on Mrs. Smith's explanation of Thanksgiving, which is something she sees as 'Canadian' and beyond the scope of the students' awareness even though all of her students have lived all their lives in Canada. This apparent lack of cultural inclusion is also revealed when discussing Christmas and her explanation of Bhangra dancing:

Mrs. Smith:	It sure does but more than that. Yes, it does. Thanksgiving does mean love but what else does it mean??
Boy:	It means you give stuff to other people.
Mrs. Smith:	Not exactly, not exactly.
Another Boy:	(quietly) You eat turkey.
Mrs. Smith:	Oh! You eat lots!! Just like Squirt does (points to back of classroom) all day long. Why? Why? Yes you do. Thanks. . .giving. Compound word. (gestures) Thanks. . .giving. What do you give?
Students:	Thanks.
Mrs. Smith:	Give thanks. Give thanks for what??
Boy:	Stuff that you have.
Mrs. Smith:	Aaah! Stuff that you have. You can give thanks for your computer, your Nintendo 64, your Sony Playstation, your food,

your books, your clothes, your toys, your animals, even your baby brother (voice breaks down in mock-weeping) or baby sister. . .

(Class laughs and agrees)

Mrs. Smith: Oh! That's a toughy!! For all the love that grandma gives you and all the love that grandpa gives you--you give. . .Thanks! You give thanks. Why do we eat when we're giving thanks?? Why do we eat when we're giving thanks??

Boy: Turkey?

Mrs. Smith: Why? Why? Why? Because it's easier to give thanks when everybody's all together isn't it? When everybody is all sharing-- sharing food, sharing company, it's much easier to give thanks. Do you know what happened years and years and years and years ago that started all this THANKSgiving??

Boy: There was a person -----?

Mrs. Smith: (points purposefully) Over in England. Some people sailed on a boat, a Mayflower boat and they sailed across the ocean and when they got on land over here they didn't know how to do very much because there wasn't houses and there wasn't food growing or anything and they thought, 'Oh! How are we going to live? How are we going to work? How are we going to do anything??' And Indians were already living here and they said, 'Ho! Look at those guys; they don't know anything. We'll help them. We'll show them how to plant things, we'll show them how to cut trees, we'll show them how to make log cabin houses, we'll help them.' And the people who sailed on the little boat, the pilgrims, said, 'You know--those Indians have been awful good. They've been RRREAlly good; we want to say Thank you. So we'll have a BIG dinner-party for them and we'll say, 'Come on, come on, come on to our houses that you helped us build; come on and share the food that you helped us grow and we will say Thank you, we will say Thank you because you've been SO good to us. Because you've been so good.'' And that's what they did; they set up HUGE big tables and they filled them full, full, full with food and food and food and food. And they danced and they had a good time together sharing and giving thanks. Sharing and giving thanks. That's how they said thank you. So on Sunday or on Monday most people in Canada who are Canadians for sure, and some of you will be doing it too as you become a little bit more Canadian, will have a big dinner and invite either their family or their friends or grandmas, grandpas, aunts, uncles, cousins, babies, big people, little people. . .and they will have a party, an eating party and a talking party sometimes even a dancing party, to say thank you. To say thank you for ALL the good things we have. . .because we have so much. And on the first sheet that you're going to get, you have to decide what you want to say thank you for. Thank you for. . .

Classroom Visit #3

The teacher appears to be privileging European Canadian culture. She seems unaware of the reality that her Punjabi students have never lived anywhere else but Canada. Are they not also Canadian? How does she imagine them becoming 'a little more Canadian'? The 'as you become a little more Canadian' statement is a troubling one, one that reveals her view that the children are outsiders who must be initiated into the 'real' culture. This statement spoken in the classroom, not in a private interview with me, is an overt message of their exclusion from a European-Canadian ethnicity. To the teacher, these children are outsiders who, if they try hard to assimilate, may be accepted by the exclusive, desired mainstream white Canadian culture.

Also noted in this sample is the absence of 'good' language teaching. The lesson contains neither evidence of comfortable, stress-free environment nor much evidence of the vast array of questioning possibilities. There is little provision for language play or activities that would allow for a range of language functions, and there is also no language activity with peers or problem solving situations. What is also lacking is a focus on key words that could be new (such as 'ocean' or 'pilgrim'), no writing of the words on the board or repetition of key phrases. In this sense, the lesson falls short of meaningful ESL teaching practice.

Mrs. Smith continues in this next excerpt to reveal her views of Canadian culture to her students:

Mrs. Smith: ...I picked something that is a Christmas thing; that LOTS of Canadian people make for Christmas. And I picked it without

	eggs. If you look at all these words, there is no egg anywhere inside. So it's going to be perfect. Is the word 'meat' anywhere?
Class:	No.
Mrs. Smith:	No. Because this is a cookie thing, not a meat thing. Okay? So this is something that moms can try to make for... a special Christmas treat, or for a special treat for another time, because they're very good. You'll find out tomorrow. What does it have in it?
Students:	Flour, water.
Mrs. Smith:	Butter.
Boy:	Icing.
Mrs. Smith:	Icing sugar. Like you make icing on top of cakes.
Boy:	Flour.
Mrs. Smith:	Flour, to hold it all together.
Boy:	Corn... starch. Starch.
Mrs. Smith:	Yeah. Cause what's that little word?
Class:	Starch.
Mrs. Smith:	Star-ch. Starch. That's what we didn't have yesterday. I had this and it's not going to work so I'll put that over there, so we don't get any in by mistake. What's this?
Class:	(shout out various things, including 'salt.')
Mrs. Smith:	Salt. And this is...?
Boy 1:	Vinegar.
Boy 2:	Vanilla.
Mrs. Smith:	Vanilla.

Classroom Visit # 4

'That moms can try' is not only gender stereotyping but, in this context, it suggests that Christmas baking is something that must be non-existent in their lives because it is white-Canadian; the teacher needs to explain the necessary element of Christmas. More than this, their mothers should be doing this baking to be initiated into Canadian culture. The assumption is that her students are not Canadians, that Christmas is Canadian, and that she, as their ESL teacher, is their source of cultural knowledge.

The excerpt also does not suggest that 'good' language instruction is taking place. The baking experience could be a good one for playing with the language and for demonstrating various language models (like recipe making).

Yet there is no suggestion that the language used is meaningful or something to be modeled. Mrs. Smith used no pictures or repetitions of key phrases and only she actually touches the ingredients; the children watch.

In this next excerpt, Mrs. Smith attempts to participate in a casual conversation with her students but there is not a clear feeling of comfort:

(Clip changes to Ally [me] standing up now, trying to do bhangra dancing, surrounded by five or six girls.)

Mrs. Smith: (off-camera) Her feet aren't moving right. What do you do with your feet, cause her feet aren't moving right. (Ally tries again.) No, no, no, no, no. There's little steps, aren't there? Little shuffles?

(One of the girls does a dance.)

Girl: Why are you laughing at us, there?

Mrs. Smith: Well, we'll kick them out! No, how do your feet go, because your feet do a little sort of shuffle.

(Some girls and Mrs. Smith all talk at the same time, can't make anything out.)

Girl: We go in a circle...

Mrs. Smith: (stepping into camera) Okay, you always go round in a circle. No, no, it's not Canadian, it's East Indian, trying to Canadianize it. You have to see it to believe it, right? (some of the girls move around, dancing) Okay, everybody has to head out now so I can place you outside. You can leave your stuff there if you want to, or you can tidy it up. Your choice. Go! Go! Go, guys! (can hear class chatting as they get ready to leave, they're all off-camera now)

Classroom Visit #7

Mrs. Smith's comment, 'it's not Canadian, it's East Indian, trying to Canadianize it. You have to see it to believe it' reveals that she sees the Punjabi culture as an exotic thing needing to be 'Canadianized'. I am not sure what she means by 'you have to see it to believe it,' a statement she directs to me. What would I not believe, the beauty of the dance? Is she implying, in front of her students, that she sees their ethnicity as bizarre and strange, something a white Canadian like myself could not fathom? But also, maybe it is rather amazing. However, Mrs. Smith may be trying to analyse the interaction and the influences of the two cultures.

In each of these three excerpts, it seems that Mrs. Smith sees her students as remote characters in the classroom and that she needs to inform them of what is Canadian. She also believes that she has real knowledge of her students and of their culture, which she seems pleased to highlight to me, the researcher in her room.

Ignoring girls

Mrs. Smith often seems to appear to ignore the girls' questions but not the boys'. In this passage, the students are at their desks and working independently on class work. When the girl asks a question, it is ignored while the boy's question is responded to:

Girl:	Mrs. Smith? Can we do these by ourselves?
Mrs. Smith:	Okay? Now, in the middle part here, in the middle part here, you have three stamps. (Slowly and loudly) You have to find the one, SY, that has the MOST the one...the BIGGEST number, MOST!! BIGGEST!! Alright? Is it a three, a seven or a five? And please circle it cause it's much easier for me to mark. Circle it?
Boy:	Nine!
Mrs. Smith:	Shh! Shh! There is no nine—there's a three, a seven, or a five!
Boy:	Where are...?
Mrs. Smith:	Right here. Okay? You have to look at me to find out where we are, okay? Alright we're in the middle. Eight, six, nine! Circle the one.
Boy:	Nine.
Mrs. Smith:	Shhh! (says boy's name) Okay and the last one in that row...five, three, four. Which one is the most, biggest!!
Boy:	Five.

Classroom Visit #2

She is also sh-shushing the boy and yet the boy continues to speak to the teacher. The sh-shushing gesture then seems to be one that may work differently with the girl (it silences her) than with the boy (it does not silence him). In this next excerpt, the girl's questions are dismissed as 'silly' or even ridiculous, while the boy's question is given due attention:

(Girl asks Mrs. Smith a question – but it is unheard by the researcher and unclear in the videotape.)

Mrs. Smith: Silly question (says name of girl), silly question! How do you think it's going to stay there?? (taps her head)

(Mrs. Smith begins moving through class and addressing students individually) Just go right...don't worry about that! Just go right... You already did that, don't worry!

(Boy asks Mrs. Smith a question)

Mrs. Smith: Hurry up and go because (begins wagging her finger at him, playfully) you were supposed to go AFTER Punjabi and Sikh studies, not now!!

(A boy approaches Mrs. Smith and asks a question) I will help you, that is what I mean!

(Mrs. Smith approaches another girl who asks her a question)

Mrs. Smith: (exclaims) Oh!! (With a teary voice) Should I get out my Kleenex?

(Girl looks up, perplexed)

Classroom Visit #2

When the boy presumably asks for permission to use the toilet, Mrs. Smith offers a slight scold for his not remembering to go earlier, yet she offers no similar connection with the girl who is told that her question is 'silly' and even gets a tap on the head. When the second girl appears, her request for attention is met with obvious sarcasm: 'Should I get out my Kleenex?' This ignoring of girls has been researched by and commented on by Zimmerman and West (1975), Spender (1980a), Corson (1993), and Lakoff (1995).

The next two excerpts again illustrate Mrs. Smith ignoring or silencing the girls' contributions. With the boys, the teacher repeats their response as a validation of their contribution.

Girl: Any side?

Mrs. Smith: Okay, can you put your sheet going up and down? Up and down. Not flat-wise but up and down? Okay? And...in the middle of that sheet we're going to try and draw an apple, okay? (draws on a large sheet of paper at the front of the class) So we sort of need a round shape and not really small...just nice... Yes, please. Where's your paper? Okay...JT (boy)! No! Okay,

	not too small because you're not going to be able to work with it if it's too tiny. Now, what does it have on top??
Boy:	A little stem.
Mrs. Smith:	A little stem so let's make a little stem on the top. And what did AR's have on it yesterday—was it yours AR?
Boy:	A leaf!
Mrs. Smith:	A leaf. Can we make a leaf on the stem?

Classroom Visit #2

Girl:	I coloured the inside.
(Other students announce that they coloured the inside.)	
Mrs. Smith:	And what colour is the leaf going to be?
Girl:	(rather gleefully) Mrs. Smith I coloured the inside.
Mrs. Smith:	Over there you know you're going to have to do it again if you weren't listening! (... 20 seconds) And the little stem, is brown. The little stem is brown. Some of you have to do it again because you weren't paying attention to what I was talking about. You were just doing whatever you wanted to do.

Classroom Visit #2

However, with a boy Mrs. Smith's response is to the point:

Boy:	Can you write right on it?
Mrs. Smith:	As soon as you get to the paper. Do not make an 'a' that way— good boy!

Classroom Visit #2

Examples of the teacher routinely praising the boys and supporting their development are numerous. Such examples of boys being privileged while the girls are silenced suggest that these girls may be constructed by their language teacher into saying nothing: the girls are gradually being silenced by a classroom that generally offers more significance to male contributions. Some boys in this room are also quiet and some girls are more talkative than others but, in light of the linguistic space measured in Charts 1 and 2, it is the girls who are generally quieter. The evidence in these few classroom moments might give a reason as to why: they tend to be ignored. This is in part because of the teacher's practice and it is a common teaching method (Flanders, 1970).

Interacting with girls through correction

In the following excerpt, Mrs. Smith is responding to student work on their Thanksgiving assignment.   To the girl, she makes explicit corrections, minimizing her efforts in many respects, by saying, 'And what is 'happing'?.' To the boy she responds with, 'Great.' The girl has received the teacher's attention but the response is corrective only, not supportive; the boy in a similar situation receives praise:

(Mrs. Smith continues to assist students individually while camera focuses onto individual students' papers)
(Mrs. Smith approaches girl's desk)

Mrs. Smith: Now. We need a period at the end of each one of these and then you can read them for me. And what is 'happing'?

Girl :   I forgot.

Mrs. Smith: (laughs) You forgot what? But it says happing which I don't know what 'happing' is. Alright. Go ahead.

(Girl begins reading and Mrs. Smith interrupts)

Mrs. Smith: Why do you put the DOT on top of the T??? Oh no. Put it down beside.

Girl :   (reading) Thank you for making the families. . .

Mrs. Smith: All right, you don't need the 'e' in there; erase the 'e,' you don't need it. Yes please, all right, thank you for the house.

Girl :   Thank you for the toilet(?).

Mrs. Smith: Got it.

Boy :   Thank you for.

Mrs. Smith: Good!

(Camera changes its focus to that of another student's paper, whom Mrs. Smith is assisting)

Boy: Thank you for a toy. Thank you for a house. . .(continues to thank for a turkey, a drink, and a book)

Mrs. Smith: Great! All right, NOW you may go.

Classroom Visit #20

Correcting in ESL, according to Krashen (1982/1995) and Chaudron (1988), is not necessary if better questioning is used instead to improve the language. Also, correcting makes for a high affective filter (high anxiety) that lowers the language development in language learners.

In the following excerpt, Mrs. Smith responds to the boys' comments but ignores the girl in the conversation that follows:

Mrs. Smith:	Okay, uniforms. Is there anyone else who does not have it on?
Boy 2:	I do!
Boy 3:	I do!
Mrs. Smith:	So that's two? All right, twenty-five take away two? You got what? All right so twenty-five...
Girl:	He's got his sweater on...
Boy 3:	He's got his shirt!
Mrs. Smith:	He's got his shirt, all right take away two... Twenty-five take away two, anybody got an idea?
Students:	Twenty-three! Twenty-three!
Mrs. Smith:	Twenty-three. Seventeen? I don't think so.
Student:	Seventeen! Who said that?

Classroom Visit #6

Arguably, the teacher is responding to the second, louder voice. Boys often trump girls who produce ideas. Each morning, one or two students participate in Show and Tell routine. Today is Zara's turn. Each student has, presumably, equal time to present a story or a special object to the class, with other students interacting with the presentation by way of guessing a hidden object. Zara has brought a Ninja Turtle toy to show. As is the routine, she begins by describing it to the class, allowing them a chance to guess at what the object might be. What is of interest is how Mrs. Smith seems to thwart her efforts, telling her immediately, 'You're talking to your bag and we can't hear you.' Other than such corrective gestures, Mrs. Smith offers little reaction to Zara's presentations. In this way, the methods the teacher uses to silence girls seem particularly prominent in her treatment of Zara. Several 'Show and Tell' moments with Zara follow:

Zara:	My thing's black and...and...
Mrs. Smith:	You're talking to your bag and we can't hear you.
Zara:	It's orange and it's black and it's white and red.
Mrs. Smith:	Wow!! Orange and black and white and red. And we don't yell out—remember we put our hand up.
Zara:	KP?

Boy:	Is it a ring?
Mrs. Smith:	Is it a ring? (Zara takes the object out of her bag) Oh! Good guess! Wow. Oh it's a...it's a...
Students:	Ninja Turtle!
Mrs. Smith:	Ninja Turtle.
Boy:	Ninja Turtle—I have . . .
Mrs. Smith:	Okay. (Zara leaves the front.)

Classroom Visit #6

(Zara comes up to the front with her back-pack for Show and Tell.)

Zara:	(very quietly) It's red with blue sparkles and it's white with brown and it's soft.
Mrs. Smith:	It's red with blue sparkles and it's white and it's brown.
Zara:	It's soft.
Mrs. Smith:	Oh! And it's soft. Mmm.

(Students put up their hands and Zara asks a girl.)

Girl:	Is it a ---?---?
Zara:	It's kind of.
Mrs. Smith:	Kind of. Alright. So you're really close.

(Zara asks a boy in the front row.)

Boy:	Is it a, uh, um, a ---?

(Zara shakes her head and pulls out a teletubby.)

Zara:	It's a teletubby.
Mrs. Smith:	Oh... and what do they do? Just cuddle?
Zara:	They show the TV on their belly.
Girl 2:	I watch that show.
Mrs. Smith:	Oh. (Zara gets up and puts her bag away.) SN (boy), would you like to tell us your favourite ----?--? Sh! Sh!

Classroom Visit #8

The teacher is attempting to support Zara by echoing her contributions and showing an interest, yet the effect of her support is not always supportive. This next excerpt suggests this possibility:

Mrs. Smith:	Okay. TI (boy), anything for sharing? GT (boy), anything for sharing? Shhh! RT (boy)! JT (boy), anything for sharing? SN (boy), anything for sharing? Well hurry up—go get it! AR

	(boy), anything for sharing? No? Zara, anything for sharing? You're going to share it later?
Zara:	I brought a baby picture.
Mrs. Smith:	Oh! No, no, no. We're ready for that later. Right? We're going to share baby pictures later. Yup, yup! We're ready for that later. All right, let's get back to our desk please and let's get back into our phonics book and find that crazy pencil, wherever it went for the night. Great. And if you could just do two for me—one here and one here.

Classroom Visit #7

Even in Zara's Show and Tell moments, it is boys who were asked for their contributions with Zara herself eliciting the boys' contributions. It is also interesting to notice that all of the Show and Tell artifacts are western and not Punjabi. In this regard, it appears that the home culture shared by all the students in this room is not particularly promoted as part of language development or of the classroom community (Gibbons, 1998).

Dismissing girls

In this other Show and Tell excerpt, Zara's attempt at participation is possibly mocked as something grade one or kindergarten children might enjoy but not a grade two child: the children laugh in response, prompted by Mrs. Smith:

Mrs. Smith:	Yeah. Mm-hmm. (Boy 1 sits back down.) Yeah. They make them just like the real ones. (Zara goes up for sharing.) Don't talk in your bag, though. Talk up, okay?
Zara:	It's white and it's red.
Mrs. Smith:	Perfect. White and red. (excitedly) Candy cane?
Zara:	(shakes her head)
Mrs. Smith:	Aahh.
Zara:	MP?
Girl:	(inaudible)
Zara:	(shakes her head)
Mrs. Smith:	Is it? Is it...? (Zara pulls out a Santa hat and puts it on.) A Santa hat! Wonderful! A Santa hat! Can I borrow it when we do singing time? With the kids? (Zara gets up, looking pleased,

and walks off-camera.) Oh, that would be so much fun! The grade ones would love it, wouldn't they?

Class: (laughing) Yeah!

Mrs. Smith: And kindergartens?

Class: Yeah!

Mrs. Smith: They would love it! Any more sharing?

Classroom Visit #13

Another interpretation to this segment is that Mrs. Smith is encouraging and recognizing Zara's contributions, even asking to borrow the hat. I, however, saw the moment as a painful one for Zara who did not engage more fully. She smiled but she did not enter dialogue. To me, Zara appeared remote and, as a result, remained as quiet as possible.

This next moment is a tender piece between Mrs. Smith and Zara. In it, Mrs. Smith quickly but deliberately recognizes Zara's mother in the midst of story-reading by announcing that some apples had been donated to the class by her mother:

Mrs. Smith: . . . Geese and chickens and a big fat turkey walk with us to the orchard where the apples and pumpkins grow.' Orchard. Orchard. 'My father picks apples. My mother does too. I climb into an apple tree and pick the reddest apples of all.' Who picks apples? Who picks apples? Zara?

Zara: My mom does.

Mrs. Smith: Right. And she sent us some apples for eating at healthy food time, with our snack-time. 'When our basket is full of shiny red apples, we go to the field where the pumpkins grow. I look and look until I find the BEST pumpkin of all. My father cuts it from the vine.'

Classroom Visit #6

This moment of recognition, something discussed in the theory of intersubjectivity as central to a language community, is only two seconds long in the whole of Zara's year with Mrs. Smith. This is brief, almost nonexistent, but nevertheless Mrs. Smith does announce that it was Zara's mother who donated the apples. And yet this is all she says; she continues to read the story to the quiet, listening students. Mrs. Smith does not say how generous Zara's mother was to donate the apples:

Mrs. Smith:	OK, some of us like it and some of us definitely don't. But anyway. Alright. So. Zara's mom goes to work every day. What does she do? (Gets up and comes back with plastic bag full of apples.)
Students:	Apples.
Mrs. Smith:	One thing she does (holds up an apple.)
Class:	Apples.
Mrs. Smith:	Zara, can you tell us what your mom does?
Zara:	My mom picks apples.
Mrs. Smith:	She picks apples. Nice BIG apples. Some of these ones have bruises, but we'll get lots of good snacks out of these ones. I went and got a different kind of apple, because those are *eating* apples, and these are *cooking* apples. You can eat these ones, they're OK, but they're a little bit sour. And what happens when you put something sour in your mouth? BT (boy). (Students scrunch their faces.)

Classroom Visit #6

The apples Zara's mother donated are ultimately dismissed as 'bruised' and Mrs. Smith takes the effort of announcing that she herself brought in more suitable apples, ones not so 'sour' and better for cooking (the activity the children are about to engage in). It is difficult to know how Zara might feel at this moment. It is reasonable to suggest that she has chosen to be silent because the environment is not safe for her to contribute. Perhaps she did not care. Whatever the reason, Zara says nothing.

In the next piece, Mrs. Smith stops at Zara's desk after an attempt to convince one student that Punjabi people do not use bibs, and she questions Zara's work:

Mrs. Smith:	That's easy. Alright. Number 8. DN, how about you try this one.
Boy:	A baby wears this. What is it?
Mrs. Smith:	That was a bib, 'member we were trying to learn what that is? Because Punjabi people don't use it, but Canadian people use it lots.

Boy: I use it.

Mrs. Smith: Some people do, but basically you don't. So that's a bib, goes around your neck, right. Keeps your clothes all neat and clean and tidy. Alright, Zara.

Zara: I---

Mrs. Smith: Ball.

Zara: Ball with it. What is it?

Mrs. Smith: What is it?

Class: Mitt.

Mrs. Smith: A mitt. Not a mitten. A mitten goes on your hand for wintertime. This is just a mitt. Now, print the words on the line. OK? Print the words on the line. OK? Don't forget your hanger-downers, sticker-uppers, or whatever. (stops at Zara's desk) What is that? What is that word?

Zara: (inaudible, but she's obviously made a mistake.)

Mrs. Smith;   Alright. That is not what it says. (Walks away.)

Classroom Visit #6

Do Punjabi people not use bibs on their babies? That they do not seems a strange thing to have said, especially when a Punjabi student suggests that they do. Again, Mrs. Smith appears to be saying sweeping things about the children's ethnic group. When Mrs. Smith approaches Zara's desk, she asks, 'What is that? What is that word?' The buckling of Zara is painful to watch on the video. At times, the teacher appears dismissive of the girls in general in her class and is particularly uninterested in Zara's attempts to participate in the classroom: she creates a high rather than a low affective filter (Krashen, 1982/1995). Also, the teacher offers little language opportunity here: there is little evidence of a comfortable learning environment or provision for frequent interactions with Zara (Gibbons, 1998).

However, there are moments when Mrs. Smith responds kindly to the girls' comments as this next excerpt demonstrates:

Boy: Do you write the word or do you draw a picture?

Mrs. Smith: . . .what? Thank you for what? Thank you for what? and thank you for what? Good question, do you write the word or do you draw a picture? You may choose. If you want to write the word go ahead. If you want to draw the picture, go ahead. (slowly) You may choose what you want to do.

Girl: Do you have to colour it?

Mrs. Smith: You do not have to colour, no, that's a good question. You do not have to colour it if you do not wish to. BUT when I ask you to read it, you have to know what you draw or drew, I mean. You have to know what you drew. . .okay? Because you're going to be reading it for me even though there's a picture there. Okay? When you're finished, I will put colour turkeys on my chair and then you may come and get this and colour on it while I am working with these ones. Okay?

Classroom Visit #3

Mrs. Smith says, 'that's a good question' to the girl but this was unusual discourse. In fact, this particular example of clear, positive interaction was one of the few I found in the year's data.

'Good' language teaching

The teaching methods used in this ESL classroom do not appear to provide a comfortable learning environment. There is also little suggestion that there are opportunities for smaller or more meaningful interaction between the students themselves. There is little evidence of structured activities for students to problem-solve or create meanings from new language models or to develop meaningful, collaborative relationships with each other. There are few opportunities for interaction between the teacher and her individual students and there is little variety around language use and questioning. However, the position of the teacher is also a constructed identity in the room and she has her own sense of agency as well as her own limitations that may be beyond her conscious control.

There are different roles teachers play in classrooms. Maguire (1993, 1997, 1998) explores the complexity of teachers' identities, including ethnicity, age, gender, and the impact of various experiences on the teachers themselves. Maguire (1993) says,

Much research into teacher education is concerned with how to 'do it better' or with comparing and contrasting particular routes on models for the preparation of teachers . . . But there are other things too (p. 270-271).

Maguire cites gender as an element of the teacher that may impact perception, career opportunities, respect, and support.   Perhaps Mrs. Smith's teacher practices are influenced by her own worries about exercising authority in the classroom and her particular situation as the only 'white' participant in the room.   Mrs. Smith is not an especially seasoned teacher nor a young one and her age mixed with her particular experiences may contribute to her teaching practices and may also impact upon her sense of 'success or failure' (Maguire, 1993).

The chief point, however, is not an examination of or argument against Mrs. Smith as a person but on the nature of language teaching that is going on which might construct female speech and silence.   If the girls' ethnicity were an explanation of their silence (as some may informally suggest), then perhaps Punjabi girls would be designated by all their teachers as 'like that'.   There are two arguments against this.   First, girls are relatively silent, irrespective of ethnicity, in most studies of gender in classrooms; and, second, the girls in this study were not always silent.   The data reveals that context and teaching methods matter and that teachers, as classroom authorities, have an amazing amount of power in controlling particular experiences, including the amount and kind of language used by particular participants.

Teacher talk

The teacher's position is revealed in the words she uses.   She is clear in the interview with me that she sees the Punjabi culture as something from which the students need to be rescued, something to be corrected and that Mrs. Smith is the true Canadian in the room who can do the correcting.   She seems to view the girls in her classroom as in need of help into mainstream culture.   Others might see Mrs. Smith as confident, direct, and in control of her classroom or be critical of the attitude of assimilation as opposed to diversity.   Regardless of one's response to her, the linguistic space of the classroom is certainly hers. She seems to control the class by often ignoring her students, by interacting with them mainly through correction, and often dismissing them out of hand. In the interview, she said that she is devoted to language teaching and yet she provided little room for actual speech production on the part of her students, particularly that of the girls.

What may be missing in this language classroom is an understanding of intersubjectivity between Mrs. Smith and her Punjabi Canadian students. There is evidence that the teacher does demonstrate a recognition of her Punjabi students which might contribute to selfhood as based on the forming of relationships that could produce more verbal participation. However, while she sees certain elements of their identities, she ignores others. If Lacan was right in seeing language as a powerful intersubjective structure that creates community relationships, then the classroom talk of Mrs. Smith indicates a lack of student inclusion and belonging, particularly seen in the lack of linguistic space used by the girls in her classroom. She appears not to stand in a mirror of mutual recognition or acceptance of the girls, offering instead moments of alienation and correction.

Crossley (1996) believed that intersubjectivity is when 'people can be in their unique individuality for each other' (p. 82). As the pieces of transcript reveal here, this 'unique individuality' is often absent. The girls in this classroom are not recognized as belonging but rather are objectified in the gaze of another— this 'other' being the classroom teacher. If Kramsch (1993) was correct in stating that the more similarities that do exist in a given community, the greater a sense of belonging, then the alienating views of Mrs. Smith are highly problematic. If one's ethnic identity is central to one's selfhood (Hall, 1996), and much in feminist linguistics sees gender as central in language use, then this language classroom may be offering the students little in the way of growth.

There is little talking by students in this classroom and, as particularly seen in Chart 2, there is little said by the girls in the classroom lessons. This language teacher, in her quest to be a cultural informant to her ESL students, underestimates the role the students play in the interactions. Mrs. Smith is the language teacher and yet a large portion of her students say very little. It may be her own attitudes and teaching practices that keep the girls so quiet. The girls are saying so little because the boys in this room may be allowed a different and privileged language learning experience. The boys clearly take up a greater amount of the linguistic space and, as a result, they have more language opportunities than the girls. These opportunities appear, partly at least, provided for the boys by their teacher. In certain ways, Mrs. Smith does not appear to use 'good' language teaching practices of questioning, creating a comfortable learning environment, providing comprehensible input, or creating frequent opportunities for interaction between herself and her students and rarely with the girls.

In response to the research questions: yes, there is a gendered use of linguistic space in this language classroom. An analysis of the speech acts of classroom lessons suggests that the language practiced in this classroom, particularly on the part of the teacher and her teaching practices, may be constructing the girls' silence.

6

Girl Talk

The central idea in this chapter is its analysis of Zara's classroom talk seen in ordinary day-to-day classroom interactions where speech and silence are constructed into being. Classroom moments may reveal experiences that are heavily influenced by being a Punjabi girl. As discussed, Mrs. Smith appears to dominate the classroom speech. But Mrs. Smith is not all that remarkable in her routinely privileging the boys, offering response and recognition of their contributions, while regularly diminishing the girls' contributions; this behavior is often seen in teacher-led lessons (Mahony, 1985; Thornborrow, 2002).

However, Mrs. Smith's particular lack of interest in Zara highlights her lack of interest in the girls in general. It is my contention that Zara's speech and silence are being constructed in her language classroom through the language patterns around her, including that of her teacher. The language that surrounds Zara is pervasive, spontaneous, and functional in naturalistic talk; that is, the language appears without a researcher's prompts. I seek here to track the particular female speech strategies Zara herself uses (hesitations, being interrupted, and holding the floor). In other words, Zara speaks in certain ways or rather, more often than not, she does not speak at all.

Whether particular contextual details (such as who is present) have an effect on how Zara engages in classroom conversation remains a question that can partly be addressed by careful analysis of the data. It is with this in mind that the following analysis of individual gendered speech strategies is conducted. The task of this analysis is comprised of the following aims:

1 to identify any typical, recurrent discourse structures in Zara's speech;

2   to interpret the possible functions of the identified strategies in relation to the tasks in each conversation;

3   to connect meaning to Zara's classroom interaction through the identification of her use of speech; and

4   in the case that there may exist systematic patterns, to hypothesize about the possible meanings by considering the classroom context in which the conversations are situated.

In this research, I have used an 'ethnography of speaking' model (Cameron, 2001).

Conversation with girls

In this first sample, Zara and a group of girls have just finished their morning lessons and have been dismissed for recess.   However, because of rainy weather, the class has been kept in for the fifteen-minute break rather than being permitted to go outside. The girls are all eating their snacks. They have gathered around one girl's desk where I am crouched down beside her, looking at her family album. At the beginning, there are only three girls in the conversation though this shifts to include all nine girls in the class (one remains close by seated at her desk). Zara appears in the right corner of the frame. Girl 1 has brought this album to show the class as part of the Social Studies unit, 'All About Me.' I have not had opportunity to see any of the students' family pictures because such discussions will occur after I have already left for the day. Mrs. Smith suggested I ask to look at the album which I am doing in this excerpt. I am eager to see this girl's family pictures; I am looking at the album, turning pages and asking questions. Zara stands next to me and appears to take great delight in being near me, occasionally touching my shoulder. She does not, however, actively contribute.

(Camera is focused on the family album.   The camera pans in and out throughout the conversation, revealing various participants including Zara who is wearing a white salvar and kamise and her hair is in one long plait. She is in the right foreground.)

Ally:	Which one's your mom in this picture?
Girl 1:	Here.
Ally:	Is that your dad in that picture? that one? No?
Girl 1:	That's my brother's dad.

Ally:	Ok to pick up the pace a bit? Go a bit faster? ((I say this to the teacher who has indicated that she wants to leave for her coffee break)) Are they dancing Bhangra?
Girl 2:	Yeah. Her birthday's in August.
Ally:	How do ... how do you dance Bhangra?
Girl 1:	I don't know.
Ally:	Is that what they are dancing?
Girl 2:	Yeah.
Ally:	How does it go? How do you do it? Show me.
Girl 3:	I don't know how to
Ally:	You don't you don't dance Bhangra? No?
	(giggles—all girls)
Ally:	Do you can you show me? Show me how you... Why are you giggling? Can you? Can you show me? Come on.
Girl 2:	I do but I'm not going
Ally:	Ah, come on. I'll do it, too. If you show me, I'll dance too.
Girl 2:	First you do it, then I'll do it.
Girl 1:	You go first.
Ally:	OK. I think it goes like this.
(I stand and do a mock dance. The girls giggle. No one joins in.)	
Ally:	Yeah? Is that right?
Girl 2:	You dance.
Ally:	Is that ok? No? Show me. Please? So they're dancing Bhangra. OK. So the arms ... yeah? Like that? Sort of?
Girls:	No.
	((One girl begins to demonstrate))
Ally:	OK. Sort of? Show me. I'll follow. I'll follow what you do. What you do, I will do.
Teacher:	Be careful when you say that.
Girl 2:	She did it.
Ally:	Bhangra. Bhangra. ((I demonstrate again.)) They're dancing Bhangra.
Girl 4:	Bhan-agra.
Ally:	Bhangh-a-rah.
Girl 4:	Bhangra.
Ally:	Bhangra.
Girl 4:	Bhangra.

Ally: Bhangra.
Girl 4:   Bhangra.
Ally: Bhangra.
Girl 4:   Bhangra.
Ally: Bhangra.
Girl 2:   P.
Ally: Bhangra.
Girl 4:   Bhangra.
Girl 2:   p.p.
Ally: Bhangra.
Girl 4:   Bhangra
Ally: Bhangra.
Girl 4:   Bhangra
Ally: Can you dance Bhangra? ((I ask Zara, touching her shoulder.))
Girl 1:   Yeah, she knows it.
Ally: Show me. show me how to do it. I need some lessons. How can I know?
Girl 2:   We have Bhangra lessons.
Ally: Really? Where do you go for
Teacher: They don't dance that fast.
Ally: No? It isn't that fast?
Teacher: I haven't seen anything that fast.
Girl 2:   At another Punjabi school
Ally: Where is that Punjabi School?
Zara: I know where it is.
Girl 2:   It's by the...and they're big and they're somewhere there
Ally: And you go there just to learn Bhangra dancing?
((Girl 2 nods))
Ally: And do boys . . . do b ...can men and women dance Bhangra or just . . . ?
Girl 2:   Womens tell us how to do it, then they make us learn it, and get a trophy at the end.
Ally: So you really know how. You could show me.
Girl 2:   And we have to dance on the stage.
Ally: Show me a little bit. What kind of music? What kind of music?
Girl: Why?
Ally: I just want to know.

Girl 2:	We have the music at the--
Girl 5:	If you go outside, I'll try--
Ally:	Oh, I'll go. You'll show me if I go outside? And when do you dance Bhangra?
Girl 4:	Bhangra
Ally:	Bhangra. Is there—is it everyone dances at the same time or a man and a woman dance together or a man and a man or women and women.
Girl 1:	Mans can dance and womans can dance.
Girl 2:	They get in a line, right? And
Girl 5:	in a circle. a circle
Girl 2:	and they do that same stuff as umh our teacher. Um, we have a Bhangra teacher at all our classes. There is two.
Ally:	So anybody at a birthday party can dance Bhangra?
Girl 2:	Yeah
Ally:	Brothers, sisters?
Girl 2:	My brother doesn't coz what if somebody sees him? He's shy.
Girl 4:	He's shy.
Ally:	How about grandma?
Girls:	No. No.
Ally:	Why not grandma?
Girl 1:	Coz they're old.
Zara:	They'll get stuck
Girl 3:	They're old.
Ally:	It's for young people
Girl 2:	My grandma, her legs.
Ally:	So it's not for ... it's for
Girl 2:	Moms and dads and kids.
Ally:	For not old people?
Girl 1:	That's my little sister
Ally:	What's her name?

Classroom Visit #6

Apart from myself, Zara shares her age and her ethnic identity with the other discourse participants. Presumably, the only differences Zara might feel with the other girls are more personal, such as personality or other individual influences. Overall, the group has a great deal in common. At first glance, I followed the contradictions within this piece of discourse. The girls begin by telling me that they do not know how to dance Bhangra yet eventually reveal that they do dance Bhangra at birthday parties and that two of them take lessons and even compete for trophies. One girl (Girl 4) is very concerned that I pronounce 'Bhangra' correctly. Essentially, the girls indicate that they do not know how to dance Bhangra; then that they do dance Bhangra; that they do not want to show me; then they do want to show me (if we go outside); that only the young can dance Bhangra; then that the shy do not dance Bhangra. Though such seemingly contradictory truths appear rather delightful and charming (the conversation is a light-hearted and joyous one), a closer look at the conversation reveals it is a site of struggle concerning who speaks and who does not.

Zara speaks very little, offering some backchannel support in two instances. She ignores my direct question, 'Can you dance Bhangra?' and permits another student to answer for her (that she does). Each girl seems attracted to the conversation to a certain extent, with more joining in as the conversation progresses and none leaving it. One girl (Girl 2) holds the floor longer and is more forthcoming regarding content, and there is much overlapping of speech.

And though Zara is a quiet participant, she is certainly not the only one. Several of the girls say little or nothing at all. Even when the more outspoken Girl 2 attempts to involve the others in the conversation, they remain reticent and reluctant to speak. It would be interesting to know how this conversation might have progressed without me: the white Canadian adult to govern the discourse. However, my white, adult presence in this conversation could be not all that different from conversations engaged in with Mrs. Smith (who marginally participates in the conversation from off the frame). But clearly it is. These seven-year old girls are presumably in a comfortable classroom setting: this is not a formal lesson; they are on their break; I am not their teacher; they are not required to remain or to participate (but they all do—some by speaking and others by watching). I am still a figure of authority, asking questions in a teacher-like way. There is a lot of self-consciousness, especially at the beginning, though the girls loosen throughout the conversation. In many ways, they hold the power of information to my ignorance concerning Bhangra. In this sense, there is more intersubjectivity, more mutual recognition, than seen in the classroom talk involving Mrs. Smith.

The strands of evidence may imply that Punjabi female language learners may be reluctant speakers even in casual, friendly conversations involving females;

Zara is an effective watcher or listener of interactional discourse and appears to be hesitant to engage in speaking acts. Such indications mean much to language educators. If language teachers interpret the reticence of some female language learners to mean inability or lack of confidence, they may be wrong. Various ways of participating in conversation, including silence, appear often in Zara and other girls in the class. The speaking that occurs in this classroom is influenced by the way the relations exist with Mrs. Smith and the particular behavior of any given student. Even in this sample of talk in her classroom with those of the same gender, same age, and same ethnic group, Zara does not speak; perhaps, then, she is not a speaker. Such an admission does not mean she cannot participate, for she does, but that she does not often speak. If Zara was in a classroom community of a more diverse nature she might also not speak. A language teacher might interpret such silence or shyness as something to do with her role as an outsider—that her ethnicity might explain such reserve. This could be a mistake.

But Zara's participation in this setting suggests that, while she is a quiet participant in classroom talk and that the role of female speech in a second language learner might account for speech acts in certain settings, it does not explain her virtual silence in a more relaxed and friendlier setting such as this one. Zara's silence is explained in different ways by the work of Spender (1980a) and Lakoff (1995). She is silent and, as evidenced in the teacher's dismissal of her, she is also possibly constructed into this silence. The classroom environment does not provide her with many opportunities to speak and, as an often-quiet girl, she does not appear to initiate opportunities for doing so.

Female speech tendencies

This section isolates and presents the classroom talk of Zara using female speech tendencies explored in the linguistic literature.

Hesitations

Mrs. Smith: Some people do, but basically you don't. So that's a bib, goes around your neck, right. Keeps your clothes all neat and clean and tidy. Alright Zara.

Zara: I---

Mrs. Smith: Ball.

Zara:	Ball with it. What is it?
Mrs. Smith:	What is it?
Class:	Mitt.
Mrs. Smith:	A mitt. Not a mitten. A mitten goes on your hand for wintertime. This is just a mitt. Now, print the words on the line. OK? Print the words on the line. OK? Don't forget your hanger-downers, sticker-uppers, or whatever. (stops at Zara's desk) What is that? What is that word?
Zara:	(inaudible, but she's obviously made a mistake.)
Mrs. Smith:	Alright. That is not what it says. (Walks away.)

Classroom Visit #6

It is Zara's use of 'I---' and her admission of uncertainty after offering her answer of 'ball' that I have itemized as hesitation. She immediately offers 'What is it?' and is corrected by Mrs. Smith and then ignored.

In this next excerpt, Zara hesitates and is responded to with correction:

Zara:	My thing's black and…and…
Mrs. Smith:	You're talking to your bag and we can't hear you.
Zara:	It's orange and it's black and it's white and Smith and red.
Mrs. Smith:	Wow!! Orange and black and white and Smith and red. And we don't yell out—remember we put our hand up.
Zara:	KP?
Boy:	Is it a ring?
Mrs. Smith:	Is it a ring? (Zara takes the object out of her bag) Oh! Good guess! Wow. Oh it's a…it's a…
Students:	Ninja Turtle!
Mrs. Smith:	Ninja Turtle -----.
Boy:	Ninja Turtle—I have -----.
Mrs. Smith:	Okay. (Zara leaves the front)

Classroom Visit #6

In the following clip, Zara tries to be clear with her words but is dismissed by her teacher.

(Zara comes up to the front with her backpack for Show and Tell.)

Zara: (very quietly) It's red with blue sparkles and it's white with brown and it's soft.

Mrs. Smith: It's red with blue sparkles and it's white and it's brown.

Zara: It's soft.

Mrs. Smith: Oh! And it's soft. Mmm.

(Students put up their hands and Zara asks a girl.)

Girl: Is it a ---?---?

Zara: It's kind of.

Mrs. Smith: Kind of. Alright. So you're really close.

(Zara asks a boy in the front row.)

Boy: Is it a, uh, um, a ---?

(Zara shakes her head and pulls out a teletubby.)

Zara: It's a teletubby.

Mrs. Smith: Oh... and what do they do? Just cuddle?

Zara: They show the TV on their belly.

Girl 2: I watch that show.

Mrs. Smith: Oh. (Zara gets up and puts her bag away.) SN, would you like to tell us your favourite ----?--? Sh! Sh!

(Girl gets up and sits in the seat in front of class.)

Classroom Visit #8

The seeming constant correction by Mrs. Smith in this next excerpt demonstrates Zara as hesitating while reading aloud her assignment to Mrs. Smith. Her hesitation seems a reasonable response to the reactions of her teacher:

(Clip changes to Mrs. Smith checking over Zara's work.)

Mrs. Smith: She. She...

Zara: ...was walking.

Mrs. Smith: Walk-ing. (erases and writes something)

Zara: ...walking on the street. There was a man hiding...

Mrs. Smith: Hidden... oh, hiding (erases and fixes it). Just 'ing.' Remember, we don't need to keep the 'e' in 'hiding.'

Zara: Hiding in the trees. Then the man shot the...

Mrs. Smith: Shot. Shot. (erases and fixes it) Ooh, this is a good guy and a bad guy, isn't it? The...

Zara: The ---?--- and the girl died.

Mrs. Smith: Aaah. Uh. Alright. There we go. Okay. Okay.

Classroom Visit #9

When Zara speaks with me in the next piece of classroom talk during playtime in 'the house', I ask her the name of the doll she is holding. She offers a one-word response ('Huh'?). Her lack of engagement seems to invite other girls to join in the conversation instead:

Ally: I guess you feel it when he's going to jump. ...Yeah, I'm in the way. (Ally gets up and organizes her things. Zara, Girl 2, and a third girl are chatting and playing in the background. Ally goes over to Zara, who is holding a doll in one hand and a baby crib in the other.) Okay, so what's your daughter's name?

Zara: Lisa.

Ally: Lisa. Lisa. That's a nice name. How did you come up with that name?

Zara: Huh?

Ally: How did you come up with that name?

Zara: Uh... (doesn't respond; she and Girl 2 continue playing)

Ally: Does Lisa sleep a lot?

Zara: Yeah.

Ally: Yeah? Is she a sleepy baby? Because some babies aren't really sleeping babies; some babies are always, you know, crying and punching. (Zara is clearly more interested in what she and Girl 2 are playing, than in this conversation.) What are you doing? Are you making supper? What's for supper?

Girl 2:   Soup.

Ally: Soup. For Lisa.

Girl 2:   Yeah.

Ally: Yeah. Does she have any food allergies?

Girl 2:   (shakes her head)

Ally: No.

Girl 2:   I have.

Ally: Do you?

Girl 2:   I have allergies.

Ally: Yeah? To what?

Girl 2:	I don't know. (Zara walks away.)

Classroom Visit #9

Zara tries to interact in a classroom discussion in the next example but her contribution is ignored. Interestingly enough, she is the only girl to attempt to contribute here:

Mrs. Smith:	Because I know that's our favourite, so I brought some of those in. Okay. And we still have to decide how to pass the...?
Class:	Competition! Competition!
Mrs. Smith:	(gets up and counts something behind her) 1-2-3-4-5-6-7-8- to the people who haven't got them yet.
Class:	Competition! Competition!
Mrs. Smith:	It's gonna... We can't race in here. It's too small.
(Students shout out various things, all at once.) Sh!	
Boy:	We have straws, right, and we put little papers and whoever's goes the farthest, you blow in it, and whoever's goes.
Boy:	It doesn't go that way.
Mrs. Smith:	That's lovely, but I don't want that mess in my room!
Class:	(laughs)
Mrs. Smith:	Ewww! That would be fun, though.
Zara:	You could get a bean bag and um, you could put the bean bag higher and ---?--- the candy cane.
Boy:	Everyone...
Mrs. Smith:	Because we got it from here all the way to the door. We were firing the bean bag at the door the other day. From back here and many kids got it.
Boy:	I want...
Mrs. Smith:	... But the door opened and a dad looked in, and he ran. He didn't like what we were doing. But we were having so much fun.
Boy:	(suggests something involving a balloon)
Mrs. Smith:	We don't have many balloons, and if you blow them that hard, you're going to scare yourself silly.
Class:	(laughs)
Mrs. Smith:	Really. But tomorrow, should we play the balloon game?

Class:	(excitedly) Yeah!
Mrs. Smith:	We'll need to check and see how many more balloons we need, so that everyone can have one. Okay? And then I'll buy that many.

Classroom Visit #13

Zara's contribution is not noticed: she may, as a result, be constructed into further silence. The boys also get the short-shift here; however, they seem to persist.

The following clip provides evidence of another painful interaction with her teacher; Zara is again corrected and, in this excerpt, offers only minimal responses to her teacher's corrections and questions:

Mrs. Smith:	Okay. Because usually, you can't sit still THAT long. And you know your brother doesn't sit still that long. We figured that one out, didn't we? (writes in Girl's book and goes back to Zara) …Alright. (very condescendingly) When I spell a word for you, could you please copy it properly? (erases Zara's work) Alright, how long do you think you played around and whatever? Were you out in the yard or anything yesterday?
Zara:	Oh, yeah.
Mrs. Smith:	How long?
Zara:	Uh…
Mrs. Smith:	(staring elsewhere) An hour? Hour and a half?
Zara:	Yeah.
Mrs. Smith:	An hour and a half? Alright, so put 90 minutes. It's usually 5 and 19, 11 (?)
Zara:	It's on Wednesday.
Mrs. Smith:	I'm just finishing up Tuesday (and walks away to next student.

(Mrs. Smith continues circulating through class, working out activity times. Students work silently at their desks. Camera zooms in on Zara, who rocks back and forth in her chair. She turns around and calls over a girl sitting behind her. This girl comes over and helps Zara for a few seconds and then walks off. Zara starts working on her exercise again.)

Classroom Visit #23

In one moment of conversation with a boy, Zara hesitates when he asks her a question. She ultimately reveals nothing:

(Camera pans over to Zara, who talks with the boy in front of her.)

Zara:	A...
Boy:	Bike.
Zara:	A sock, with rocks. Rocks.
Boy:	Fox rhymes with rocks.
Zara:	That doesn't make any sense.
Boy:	What shirt is that for? (pointing to her t-shirt)
Zara:	What?
Boy:	What did you get that shirt for?
Zara:	Well, um...

Classroom Visit #27

Zara's one word response in this next clip is met with passing interest in Mrs. Smith:

Mrs. Smith:	Alright. Name another noun. Any noun at all.
Zara:	Zebra. (looks very pleased with her suggestion)
Mrs. Smith:	How do we get more than one? What do we say?
Class:	Zebras.
Mrs. Smith:	Zebras. Zebras. Alright. That works fine.
Boy:	Lion.
Mrs. Smith:	Lion? Alright, how do we get more than one?
Class:	Lions.

Classroom Visit #28

Zara's 'sharing' in this next classroom moment again demonstrates her hesitant speech:

(Students sort out who's doing what. A boy gets up and shares something about going to a wading pool; another boy shares his book of 'A Bug's Life'; a girl shares a toy that blows bubbles; Zara gets up and tells a story.)

Zara: Um, uh, on Tuesday, I was, uh, at the store. It was Canadian Tire and my brother saw this, a baseball and then he started to bounce it, and then, um, my dad was calling my brother, and

	then, um, uh, when he was bouncing, my brother was bouncing the ball, and you know that fishing that where you catch fishes in?
Mrs. Smith:	A net?
Zara:	Yeah. And it went in there and then my brother went to my dad and then they both went like that and then I tried to, um, pull it down, and then the ball just came out.
Mrs. Smith:	Was it a basketball?
Zara:	No, uh, a baseball.
Mrs. Smith:	I didn't think baseballs bounce.
Zara:	No, uh . . .
Mrs. Smith:	A volleyball.
Zara:	Uh, yeah (nods).
Mrs. Smith:	Ah, cause I'm not sure. A tennis ball? A little Smith thing?
Zara:	Yeah. Yeah, that one. (gets up and walks off)
Mrs. Smith:	Okay. Cause I don't think baseballs bounce. But those little guys do. The tennis balls do. They go all over the place.
Boy:	A soccer ball does.
Mrs. Smith:	Yeah, but she knows what a soccer ball is. It must be a ball that she's not, uh, sure of. Great. Okay. If you have this star sheet, could you put it in here, please? If you have field-trip money, could you bring it over there? If you have library books that you're finished with, can you put them in here? Can you go get a pencil?

(Students get up and organize themselves.)

Classroom Visit #29

These segments of classroom talk involving Zara reveal that she does use hesitations and pauses as well as hedges such as 'kind of,' 'no, uh...,' and 'oh yeah...' to contribute to conversations and, perhaps as a result, there appears a lack of genuine or meaningful engagement either by her or with her in any real discussions. More often than not, she is ignored by the other members of her class, led at least in part by Mrs. Smith.

Interruptions

In several conversations with classmates, Zara's speech appears to be interrupted and, therefore, may indicate less of a right for her to speak. These next four excerpts demonstrate such a speech pattern. All four are small group moments with other girls in her class:

(Camera focuses in on two girls playing cards; one of the girls is Zara. Both girls hold up cards and it appears the higher card will win.)

Girl: Put them back.

Zara: In the middle. Let's just...

(Shown cards again)

Zara: One again.

Girl: Yeah! Oh...Yes... Ah... (Each time showing cards)

Zara: Wait...

Girl: Hee ha! Oh you get it.

(Ding)

Girl: Oh... that scared me. You get it. Faster. I win it. I win it. I win it.

(Zara throws the cards in her lap and leaves after two minutes of the card game.)

Classroom Visit #2

This next section is one of Zara's longest interactions in the data. As such, I present it fully here. Zara is playing cards with one other girl in class during free-time. The conversation contains some full sentences but mainly one-word responses and discontinued or interrupted phrases:

(Camera changes to focus on Zara and Girl)

Zara: (reaches down for a card): I want to shuffle them now.

Girl: 13, 14, 15, 16, 17, 18, 19, 20. I've got twenty, hurry up! (bossy, commanding)

Zara: Nineteen! (smiles)

Girl: (Deals more cards.) One is extra. Put this in this zip-lock--it's your duty.

Zara: And tomorrow I'm... (gets distracted/intimidated because Girl looks away. Zara loses the attention of Girl and discontinues her sentence.)

Girl: Ready?

Zara: (quietly) Yup.

Girl: Just wait! (bossy)

Zara: Can I go first?

Girl: Sure. Put this down here. (bossy/commanding)

(Girls put cards down in the middle)

Girl: What one do you got? You got six?

Zara: Six.

Girl: So we have to put one in the middle. No you can't choose one
               now, you've already chosen that number.

(Zara holds up a card)

Girl: (whispers) Six. . .

Zara: Don't keep shuffling them! (commanding!)

Girl: I'm not, I didn't shuffle them. . .

(Girls continue to play by holding up cards and deciding which gets to keep
both of them)

Zara: I get it. I'm gonna shuffle them now.

Girl: I thought you said that you weren't.

Zara: No I didn't!

Girl: Whatever. You said that's your last one--so now who shuffles?
               (Both girls have been actually saying something that sounds
               more like 'shoveling' the whole time but is best interpreted as
               'shuffling.')

(Girls continue to play for a while in relative silence)

Girl: Eight. Five.

Zara: Put them on the ground. I like to pick them up. This is my card
               and this is your card. OK? I like to do it like that.

Girl: No. Put them down.

Zara: Don't keep shuffling the cards (commanding)

(Girls finish the game—giggling.)

Zara: Hey. I'm going to put 'em by myself.

Girl: OK. Count.

Zara: I'll pass them out.

Girl: No! I told you! I told you--I get to pass them out!

Zara: Tomorrow I'm going to pass them out.

Girl: Fine. Tell me what is -----. (repeats several times)

Zara: What??

Girl: What is yeash??

Zara: Yeash??

Girl: Shuffle. What is yeash?

Zara: I don't know.

Girl: It means: (makes a face) Duh! Don't you even KNOW
               something??

(Zara slowly shuffles cards)

Girl: I didn't say that to you; I just said that Yeeeeeash...but really
               yeash means that you don't know anything but I'm just
               pretending to say it to...someone...Yeash!!! (points and says
               quietly:) Look!

(Girls both look at another student and then Girl deals again.)

Girl: One. Two. Three. Four.

Classroom Visit #3

Zara seems a lot more comfortable and confident in this one-to-one interaction
with this particular girl than in a full classroom situation. Although she is less
dominant than Girl 1, Zara interacts naturally with her partner throughout the
game. She even protests quite strongly at a couple of points when she's
unhappy with her partner's behavior. The other girl speaks marginally more
often and for greater lengths of time. But even in this girl's speech, short
phrases persist. The conversation is not a particularly friendly one and does
not seem to portray a genuine, happy time of play between friends. At one
point, the girl asks Zara, 'Duh? Don't you even know something?' though she
quickly attempts to retract this.

In this way, Zara is kept out of classroom conversations, even ones which
involve her directly. More often seen, however, are conversations where Zara
begins to contribute but is cut off by her teacher and her contributions are
incomplete as a result. The next segment centres on a brief classroom
conversation about Chinese New Year and the various animals in the Chinese
zodiac:

(Camera pans over to Zara)

Girl: You know when I was born? The year I was born? 1992.

Zara: I was born in 1992, too. I was too. (excited!)

(Girl says something to Zara)

Zara: Yeah! I was born on the third too. Mrs. Smith! I was born in
               1992 and I was -----. (very humble and intimidated in her
               approach)

Mrs. Smith: That would be a different animal if you were born in 1992.

Girl:	We were both the same.
Zara:	She was born...and I was...
Mrs. Smith:	All right—how are we doing? Have we got those animals sort of out and about now?

Classroom Visit #18

The following clip is rather muddled, a brief moment at Zara's desk when she interacts with Girl 2. The communication seems relatively insignificant, superficial, yet, by the end, Zara attempts to articulate herself and defends her mistake:

(Clip changes to Zara, at her desk, with Girl 2 and Girl 3 in the background. Zara says something to them under her breath, turns around and goes back to work. She sticks her tongue out and wipes her nose rather dramatically. She plays with her hair, rests her head on her hand, and then asks for her eraser back. Girl 4 drops it on her desk.)

Zara: My eraser, [uses the diminutive of Girl 4's name].

(Girl 2 comes over to Zara's desk, wanting to fix her work for her.)

Girl 2:   Just let me fix everything, okay? This one's kind of broken. (Zara leans over and covers up her work, giving Girl 2 the clear impression she doesn't want her help.)

Girl 2:   (defensively) I'll just put a little piece of tape on it; it's broken. (apologetically) I was just fixing it. (Zara doesn't budge.) Fine. (Girl 2 turns away and sits back down at her desk. Zara stares off for a few seconds and then continues her work, reading aloud as she writes. Music plays from somewhere, and she is clearly distracted for a few seconds. She gets back to work, with her head against the desk. After a few seconds, she flips her work over, gets up and walks off. The camera follows her over to where Mrs. Smith is helping some students and then quickly back to her desk again. She reads over her work aloud for a few seconds and then stares off in various directions.)

Zara: (to Girl 2--asks her a question)

Girl 2:   Gifts.

Zara: Gifts.

Girl 2:   Gifts. I like getting presents.

Zara:	Teddy bear! (to herself in a sing-song voice) I put pencils in my hair. (chuckles; reads titles of books at the front of the room) Duck, duck, goose. Teddy bear, teddy bear. The ant and the elephant. (under her breath) The Three Little Pigs. Baby... Well, well, we ate the ---?---. We were ---?---. (to Girl 2) Where's my pencil? (She has stuck her pencil through her hair.)
Girl 2:	(reaches over and pokes the pencil) Right there.
Zara:	(leans back and laughs. She puts the pencil back in her hair and asks Girl on other side of her.) Where's my pencil?
Girl 1:	Right here. (pulls it out and puts it on Zara's desk) Right here.
Zara:	(angrily) Don't. I'm gonna tell on you. I'm telling on you. (sighs, gets up and sits back down again. After a few seconds, she asks Girl 2 for help.) ... I don't... How do you do this? I 'ust' go to school? I (laughs) ust go to school? (laughs)
Girl 2:	(condescendingly and mockingly) I bust? I MUST go to school.
Zara:	I must go to school?
Girl 2:	Yeah.
Zara:	I was going to say I must, go, I must, not bust, go to school (laughs). I... I must (writes it down and then erases something). Done. Re-read. (picks up her work, holds it up and reads it over) I must go to school, I must, I did not go to school. (laughs) I must (writing again). I must... I go on a... bus... I just be good on the bus. I just... oh-oh... just... we... just got up there. Done. (reading her sheet) I must go to school, I bust go to school, I never go to school, I do go to school (laughs). I must go home, I always go home, I always... run home. We can run very fast.

Classroom Visit #23

I am not too certain how to interpret this particular conversation of Zara and her classmate, though it does reveal interruption and a seeming lack of significance concerning her contributions. What this conversation might suggest is that language is not serving as an intersubjective tool in this instance, though it appears that Zara may be experimenting with language in her own monologue. There appears to be no real connection between Zara and her classmate; this seems displayed in the way Zara is interrupted—she is being silenced as well as colluding in this role for herself.

Holding the Floor

Holding the floor is closely related to interruption or being interrupted. Holding the floor is to speak without interruption or to speak through an interruption on a particular topic. There are very few examples in the data where Zara appears to hold the floor. However, even when Zara attempts to contribute, her attempts are short-lived.

(Camera pans to Zara, who is sitting backwards on her chair, leaning on the desk behind her and talking to the boy in the desk. She then turns back around, picks up her scissors and gets to work cutting. Zara continues working silently at her desk for a few minutes.)

Mrs. Smith:	(off-camera) OK, if you have a minute left over and you brought your book back to trade, you can do that. Grey books right here.
Boy:	Put down my name, put down my name!
Mrs. Smith:	JT, we do not yell. OK, we do not yell all over the place.
Zara:	(to girl in desk behind her, whose work she's back observing—she hops out of her chair and points to the girl's work.) You didn't get corn.
Girl:	Huh?
Zara:	Corn.
Girl:	What?
Zara:	(assertively) That's corn. It's supposed to go there. It's pointing there!

(She sits back down at her desk.)

Classroom Visit #6

(Camera focuses on Zara)

Zara:	You just have to go like this. It's like this... You just have to go like that and then you can hold it...
Mrs. Smith:	All right—oh lots of you will need help. I can guarantee that. (gives individual instruction throughout the class)

(Camera focuses back on JT)

Boy:	(holds up his piece of macaroni) I got it!

Boy:	Hey you can't help people!
Boy:	I just picked up two. That one fell but I picked up two.

(Camera clip changes—focusing on Zara who is picking up her piece of macaroni with the chop sticks and laughing)

Zara:	KP look! (pretends to be playing the drums)
Girl:	No! You won't get it how it is.
Zara:	Huh?
Girl:	You won't get it how it...
Zara:	Yes I will—I still do. Now another one fell. Hey that's hers! (makes a sarcastic face to someone behind her. Very eager to show off her skills. Seeking approval from Mrs. Smith) Lookit! I've got it. This is how you do it! Yours fell! (drops the macaroni on the ground and squeals)

Classroom Visit #18

Each of these excerpts reveal how Zara attempts to enter the linguistic space but how she is stopped by her teacher or, at other times, seems to stop herself.

Silence

The following three excerpts are samples of classroom moments that reveal the silencing of Zara in this classroom. It is difficult to provide evidence of her silence, apart from measuring the linguistic space. But measurement can hardly account for the reasons for her silence. Initially, I selected all the sections of the transcripts that revealed Zara as present in the room. Because so much of her classroom time is spent saying nothing, such silent classroom moments were prevalent. As such, I have selected three pieces from the data that represent typical moments for Zara: that she sits at her desk, saying nothing at all, with her teacher often walking right past her or pausing only to offer correction. Is Zara quiet because of teacher practices or is she quiet because she 'just is'? Is Mrs. Smith disengaged from her because she is so quiet? Have both realities impacted each other?

(Clip changes. Class busy working quietly. Zara is helping two other girls pass out the books.)

| Mrs. Smith: | When you find the next page you'll have to start right away! The P's I want you to make the bubble first and then start the back. Remember on the d's, the little guys, you do the ball first |

and then the stick. Ball first and then the stick. Ball first and
then the stick. Then it comes out really nicely.

(Begins assisting students individually. She pauses at Zara's desk.)

Mrs. Smith: Put your name on the top. This one right here. Show me...(she
moves on)

Classroom Visit #5

(Camera pans back to Mrs. Smith helping students with their work.)

Mrs. Smith: Do not put two the same (in a sing-song voice) If you want to
trade your book, you can do that for a minute, while we just
finish up here. (Zara continues sitting patiently at her desk.)
Remember please that you pick two from here, two from here,
and then you pick one more from either space. It doesn't
matter. Whatever you want, but you need five altogether.

(Clip ends. Mrs. Smith did not check over and help Zara with her work,
though her hand was up.)

Classroom Visit #7

(Students work on their own. Camera focuses on Zara, who prints and then
erases her work. Mrs. Smith can be heard in the background, circulating
around and checking and correcting students' work. After about a minute,
camera pans out to show most students getting up and walking away from their
desks, evidently finished. Zara continues working on her own. After another
minute, Zara finishes and gets up. She never asked for help, nor did Mrs.
Smith offer any.)

(Clip changes to boy standing on his own, reading a book aloud. After a few
seconds, Mrs. Smith sings the carpet song.)

Classroom Visit #27

Zara never called out and, when addressed, she was usually corrected; she was
not listened to and certainly was rarely praised. Though she did display some
female speech patterns, her usual form of interaction was to be silent. This
supports the view of Spender (1980a, 1980b), Gal (1991), Lakoff (1995), and
Goldberger (1997), who each said that silence can be a way of disengagement
from a hostile environment and is a common female speech pattern of its own.
Girls can choose to be silent or they can be 'sh-shushed' into silence after too
many failed attempts to contribute.

Zara appeared not to be having a rich interactive experience in her language classroom. This may be partly due to the teacher's attitudes or the teaching practices in general. The teacher seemed to view Zara as an unimportant contributor and she appeared to ignore Zara on many occasions. Zara was not a particularly talkative girl in class discussions or even in smaller group talk and so she was quite easy to ignore. But this ignoring may also have caused Zara to be silent and her silence seems one reasonable response to her classroom environment. Why should she venture into more discussions when her teacher and other classmates are not supportive?

This last excerpt reveals a brief moment of revelation about the gender injustices in the classroom:

(Students all get up to hand in their homework. Lots of chatter as two boys hand out workbooks. Zara sits silently at her desk, for awhile, until...)

Zara: (to girl next to her) I don't know why the boys always do it [hand out books]. I don't care, but I'm gonna throw it. That's what I always do.

Girl 2: (says something inaudible in response)

Zara: The boys keep throwing ours down, the girls' down, when, when I'm gonna pick the girls I want, right...

Mrs. Smith: Okay, spelling books OPEN.

Classroom Visit #27

It is Zara herself, ironically, who is the one to express 'I don't know why the boys always do it [hand out books].' She is the one to ask why the boys get this privilege. This is an extraordinary thing for her to communicate. It is fascinating that it was picked up in the transcription process for it was missed in observation.

It was the intention of this chapter to explore the way a girl in a language classroom participates through examining typical, recurrent discourse patterns and interpreting the possible functions of these speech strategies within her classroom experiences. By exploring ordinary day-to-day classroom talk, gender can be seen to be a variable in linguistic experience. To what extent female speech tendencies contribute to the construction or revelation of gender is up to interpretation. Like most teachers, the teacher dominates the linguistic space and, because the girls in general take up so little of the remaining linguistic space, it was difficult to document many moments of Zara speaking.

When she does speak, she reveals some of the predictable gendered speech strategies explored in Western feminist linguistics. As such, she is in keeping with a socialized gendered self. However, her silence may be partly constructed by her teacher, by others, and also by Zara herself.

Zara's language experiences have provided some identification of recurrent discourse structures. The particular interpretation of these strategies is partially subjective and intuitive on my part but, nevertheless, it is convincing that there could be systemic forces at work in the room that create her silence. This ESL classroom experience has at least partly participated in constructing some girls of this classroom into silence and it is within this silence that one ESL girl attempts to belong by saying very little. Her few attempts to speak show her perhaps ambivalent willingness to belong but classroom practices may not be allowing her to speak. She plays her part.

It is possible that Zara may be a quiet girl in other circumstances too, or that most of the girls in this class happen to be not very talkative. This situational possibility is why single case research cannot offer generalizations to other circumstances; this is just one case. What is revealed is that classroom talk can and does construct participants to a large extent, and that gender is a powerful variable in this regard. Language teachers need to be concerned with the linguistic opportunities allowed all students. However, the linguistic choices, as Zara demonstrates, reveal that some language students may need particular attention and particular teacher practices to elicit more language use from them.

Part III

Sh-shushing Girls in Language Classrooms

7

Ethnicity and Gender: A Double Whammy

Certain views in the field of second language education remain largely assimilationist, in spite of current research suggesting other alternatives for the promotion of heritage languages in Canada (Cummins, 1985, 1993; Cummins and Danesi, 1990; Moodley, 1999; May, 2001). Gibson's (1988) study focused on a Punjabi community and highlighted a 'mismatch' experienced for Punjabi students in an American school. The possibility of a better 'match' of school and home culture that would seem to be the case for Zara in her Canadian school could provide her with better access to language use because of a recognition of ethnicity within the room. This was the hope; but this was not the case.

Despite acknowledgement of the need to belong to a community, such ethnic grouping may isolate or limit individuals because of the stereotyping emerging from such clusters anyway. The particular experience of the Punjabi Canadians is one marred by historical events and historical attitudes that developed from a shared yet different colonial experience in both Canada and India. The immigrant experience is one particularly connected to most Canadians and is a major element of Canadian society, set in a backdrop of the French-English linguistic debate. The large settlement of Punjabis in Canada summons the field of second language acquisition to explore such cultural groups concerning education and invites debate as to the reasons for such excluded school settings and the reasons against private education drawn on ethnic lines. But whether an ESL classroom is culturally specific or not, the variable of gender and its impact on language use and use of linguistic space remains a provocative one.

Also the work of Krashen (1982/1995) and Chaudron (1988), as well as numerous other researchers in the field, strongly suggest that language-learning classrooms need to be rich language-filled classrooms with a comfortable learning atmosphere and a warm relationship with the language teacher. There needs to be comprehensible input as well as acceptance. Such ESL practices did not appear in abundance in Zara's classroom.

While much work has been carried out examining the impact of gender on the classroom experience (Stanworth, 1981; Mahony, 1985) and much work written on the ethnic variable in identity construction (Hall, 1992, 1996; Rampton, 1991, 1995, 2000), less has been written about ethnicity and gender in the ESL experience, and even less in the Canadian context. It has been an aim of this project to help redress this lack in Canadian educational research. A reflection of the climate of the times, that of more inclusive policy and teacher education programs, did not produce more awareness or sensitivities of gender in this ESL classroom. Concerns regarding minority femaleness remain an important, yet unexplored, part of the classroom experience (Brah and Minhas, 1985; Bannerji, 1993, 2000; Bhopal, 1997). Without careful attention, Punjabi-Sikh girls in the primary classrooms may further slip away from ever holding 'linguistic space' (Mahony, 1985). Thus, while I have drawn conclusions about one girl and her use of English in her language classroom, a highly specific one, the account has touched on two fundamental variables in the construction of identity: ethnicity and gender. Such variables intersect.

Being the illegitimate other

This book searched for answers to two specific questions:
1 Is there evidence of gendered use of linguistic space and of gendered speech patterns in an ESL classroom?
2 If so, do such patterns in the classroom discourse suggest that speech and silence are being constructed?
The evidence suggests 'yes' to both questions, though the complexity of the classroom requires this brief summary.

The analysis of both the teacher's language use and the girls' language use revealed the critical role gender plays in behavior. The data focused on the words used by the teacher, words that possibly limited certain participation in the classroom by limiting the girls' sense of validation and legitimacy as participants. The teacher's lack of certain teaching methods further limited more verbal participation. Zara's own use of language and her use of female speech strategies provide evidence that she is learning the possibilities and limits of what she can say and how she can say it. It is her consistent use of silence that may reveal a sense of the silencing around her—that she may feel best served in this language classroom by remaining silent. Zara's speech strategies within her classroom may demonstrate a constructed gendered identity seem in her own choice to be silent. She did show attempts to speak which were often ignored. Whether it is her own active choice to be quiet or my perception of the learning environment, I am not sure.

It was clear that the girls did not have nor did they take linguistic freedom in the classroom to demonstrate their competence. Perhaps it is because of the particular ways Mrs. Smith limited participation that the girls kept low profiles in the class, and perhaps took less risk in speaking out. The girls rarely participated in conversational talk and rarely joined in on the narratives of others, often because of a lack of response from each other. This lack of recognition of their own linguistic power provides an example of how the theory of intersubjectivity may explain the complexity at work in language classrooms. That is, the girls were not particularly 'recognized' by the teacher or each other and, as a result, they failed to engage.

According to Bakhtin (1996), innovation in language is one means by which speakers can exercise their individual voice or challenge the status quo. When Zara participated in speech, she appeared limited by her teacher who may have framed or constructed Zara into a particular identity – an identity of silence. Many times Zara could not gain an audience or exert any social power. At other times, she used speech to participate. However, her silence ultimately appeared to be her most consistent speech strategy, revealed through particular classroom interactions as well as enacted by her.

The view of Mrs. Smith that Zara needed further instruction in being 'a good little girl' is problematic because the phrase implies that the uniqueness of Zara as a complex and legitimate individual is not clearly embraced by her teacher. The teacher did not appear to recognize Zara nor did she appear to create a relationship with her based on 'recognition' explained by the theory of intersubjectivity. It may be that the teacher's methods silenced Zara and limited her use of linguistic space. In addition, the power relations and unconscious emotional or affective factors seemed to be operating in this student-teacher relationship, with the teacher projecting her own images of gender and ethnicity onto Zara (that she should be quiet). In the classroom, Zara displayed marginal linguistic participation, in large part due to the lack of linguistic space allowed her as well as the teacher's response to her minor attempts at speech.

Ultimately, this classroom demonstrates that a culturally specific ESL classroom community, implicit with its shared values and possibilities for intersubjectivity, does not necessarily create a rich language learning environment. Such an observation may implicate language teacher training by suggesting that there may not be adequate emphasis placed on gender as a variable in language classrooms or on understanding of gender alongside ethnicity as a complicated mix of learner variables.

Embracing the way in which academics recently have considered gender and language, I have not regarded gender as a monolithic, fixed concept, but have attempted to account for additional contextual factors, such as the particular teacher and the particular ethnic community within Canadian society. The measurement of linguistic space available to or used by girls in this classroom revealed that the girls used almost no linguistic space in the classroom lessons: they had little linguistic space. In the few episodes where Zara spoke, she used some expected female speech patterns but ultimately she used silence either as resistance or protection. Her silence supports the view that gender is formed and reflected in the complexity of the social dynamics within each group and within each person. It is constructed. It was possible to discern some linguistic patterns in Zara's talk, though she mainly displayed a propensity to be silent. Her silence, as well as the silence of the other girls, may be an implicit requirement imposed by the teaching methods. The possible limiting of Zara's opportunities to speak should be of concern to other ESL educators who see speech as a significant avenue for learning and for producing the target language. Quite simply, ESL teaching methods could focus more on linguistic space and on who is occupying it.

This study has sought to contribute to the continuation and development of work in the fields of gender and language (Cameron, 1992, 1995a, 1995b, 1998; Coates, 1993, 1996, 1998a, 1998b); gender and education (Acker, 1994; Baxter, 1999, 2002; Corson, 1993; Holmes, 1991, 1994; Mahony, 1985, 1988; Stanworth, 1981), ethnicity and language education in Canada (Ashworth, 1992; Cummins, 1985, 1993, 1996; Fleras and Elliott, 1992; Moodley, 1983, 1999; Toohey, 1992, 1996a, 1996b, 1997, 2000); and ethnicity and gender

(Bannerji, 1993, 2000; Bhopal, 1997, Brah and Minhas, 1985). As such, I have hoped to bring together gender and ethnicity as filters of experience in language classrooms.

Gender and language

As I have argued, much of the attention in feminist linguistics has been paid to gender as impacting upon speech strategies, isolating female speakers as the marked gender, though this view is also questioned and undermined by many scholars (Connell, 1995; Cameron, 1998; Davies, 1999). However, in spite of the problems with examining female speech strategies, resting largely on essentialist views of female, there is still compelling evidence that gender (male and female) is constructed through speech and is revealed in certain speech patterns.

Early appraisals made about the deficiencies of female language or the dominant and oppressive speech of males have led to persuasive counter-arguments that female speech has been largely compared to male speech and that the same linguistic feature (such as silence) is simply interpreted differently when used by one gender over another, or that female expression cannot be valued within a patriarchal system because female speech is always interpreted as weaker. Tannen's work (1989 - 1998) suggests that males and females experience miscommunication because of different gender cultures that use different speech strategies. However, Tannen's model does not challenge sexist practices nor does she account for the way individuals use a range of styles, though she does offer a sub-cultural view at times. Generally, her work maintains a binary opposition which limits the view of individuals as complex and highly adaptive. Though the girls' use of language does, to some extent, suggest a determinism of gender because they use some 'typical' female patterns, their use of language does not support a notion of female as fixed and unchanging. Instead, the classroom talk demonstrates some female speech strategies while the argument could be made that the girls simply demonstrate speech, not necessarily female per se. The significance or rather the lack of linguistic significance of the girls as participants in the language classroom appears the most compelling part of this study.

The approach I have used in this study, which prioritizes the analysis of the experiences of girls in a language classroom, leads to an evaluation of certain interpretations of such speech. Though certain studies question whether boys really benefit from patriarchal ideologies or male speech strategies, there is some agreement that girls cannot benefit from a system that routinely silences them (Davies, 1999). Secondly, it has not been demonstrated that a girl's use of language is entirely a product of her gender in any deterministic sense. If so, the speech patterns would be consistent across contexts and they are not: the girls speak more and differently in different contexts. Their speech appears largely constructed and situated, where many elements also figure, such as personality, age, and other actors present. This study has therefore considered the learning potential as partially constructed in language use so that the use of linguistic space can be set in terms of a wider second language learning theory.

Gender and education

The approach of this research has exclusively considered talk and its relationship to gender construction in an ESL setting and has not attempted to consider other crucial elements impinging on Zara's learning experience. I acknowledge that both boys and girls learn in other ways than through spoken language (such as through writing), yet spoken language remains a valid and potent focus for understanding a classroom experience. Vygotsky (1981) and other theorists (such as Buber, 1958; Lacan, 1968) recognized that through spoken language interlocutors consciously or unconsciously enact their identities. The role of the teacher in constructing speech and silence was one in evidence here.

Generalizations cannot be made based on one example of one classroom; however, this study can contribute to larger insights and the need for a reflective classroom practice concerning ESL and gender. Mrs. Smith's classroom is one example of how connections and values exist within an ESL classroom and impact upon language use. Compelling evidence was put forward that boys occupy more linguistic space than girls. In spite of various interpretations of the amount of speech time taken up in classrooms by boys or girls, it seems evident that speech in classrooms is significant as an indicator of meaningful experience. The kind of talk engaged in by girls, and seen here in an ESL student, supports other studies that give evidence of gender in education as figuring prominently. Classrooms are 'sites of struggle' (Walkerdine, 1990; 1997). What appeared to be a struggle in this classroom was the struggle to speak at all. Such struggles need to be understood by the ESL field.

Embracing the educational and language learning values of our times, my investigation is based upon the assumption that all students need some linguistic access to the classroom discourse.   Nevertheless, it is also acknowledged that the experiences revealed here suggest a useful extension to the field of second language acquisition.   In sum, it is possible that ESL girls are regarded as girls first, rather than individuals, and therefore are expected and constructed to be quiet and cooperative in classroom contexts.

As I noted in my introductory chapter, a different ethnographer would interpret aspects of the data in different ways.   I am aware that in identifying features of speech as female, I may appear to support an essentialist way of seeing gender and speech.   Instead, I am convinced that there was evidence that Zara's identity as a girl propelled her into a certain way of being and constructed her into silence.   As a result, Zara and the other girls experienced limited access to language development in this language classroom.

Limitations of the study

This account represents interpretations of classroom events and privileges the voice of the researcher—mine.   It does not represent the interpretations of events by Zara, by her classmates, nor by Mrs. Smith.   This research, conducted in the ethnographic tradition, has pointed to the problems associated with observation and analysis of other people's interactions and behaviors.   At the same time, the problem of perspective exists in any piece of research. While the particular emphasis on the girls may be seen as a limitation of the work, this focus has allowed me to explore more deeply the complexity of being a female ESL student.

My interpretation of previous research has affected my own research stance and my ultimate analysis of the data.   The main partiality of my work can be summarized in the following points:

1   My prioritization of gender and ethnicity has meant I have not considered other crucial variables at work in this group of children's production of English;

2   The focus on the role of being female within a language classroom has meant that I have not looked at boys and the complexity surrounding their experience as socially constructed nor how their speech strategies reveal a male identity;

3   I have focused exclusively on spoken language without considering literacy or written expressions of power or gender;

4   I have used ethnographic observation and have not explored quantitative elements, other than to measure and describe the linguistic space, nor have I produced a traditional discourse analysis per se.

Data collection and selection

The method of data collection resulted in the acquisition of naturalistic material providing a rich resource for analysis. The use of a video recorder to record the classroom talk allowed for this naturalistic observation of the classroom as well as recording the teacher in interview.

My role as ethnographic observer maintained a consistent style of classroom routine throughout the year. My concentration on gender meant that, while I operated in an ethnographic manner, certain features at work in the classroom were not noticed by me: I could not see everything.

In selecting parts of the transcripts for analysis, I was aware that I had to exclude transcripts which may have placed a different emphasis on my ultimate conclusions. I made the selections exclusively on the basis of when Mrs. Smith reveals her attitudes toward gender and ethnicity and when Zara appears. In light of the hours of observation, the fact that Zara says so little speaks volumes about her marginalized participation in this classroom.

Implications of the study

As Davies (1991) notes, much research on second language learning has been undertaken from a cognitive perspective, seeing language as individual acquisition or accommodation of English. The variable of gender has been treated as highly influential in individual functioning. But recent years have seen an increase in ethnographic studies which situate learners in classroom contexts and constructed into roles by beliefs and attitudes. Important contributions have been made by critical researchers who show how power relations and social context cannot be divorced from an understanding of language use.

I examined the experiences of one classroom using intersubjectivity as the theoretical perspective connecting ethnicity, gender, and language. The data put forward suggests the helpfulness of such analysis in developing a complex understanding of what some female ESL students experienced in their classroom, and it is here that I situate my contribution. I suggest that ethnographic research into the lived experiences of ESL girls needs to take a broad framework exploring ethnicity with gender and spoken language. Such a perspective may provide useful avenues to further explore the second language learning experience. This is because such combined variables (gender, ethnicity, age) can locate the individual in relation to power (the teacher's) while emphasizing the complexity of human relationships in everyday classroom moments.

As was mentioned, linguists working in the field of gender have put forward a range of theories suggesting that the language used by females is a kind of stylized powerlessness or intentionally weak and deficient. Such arguments are countered by feminists who argue that language itself may be responsible for disempowering female speakers, while others blame patriarchy in particular. Others still account for gender variation in terms of benign difference where no blame is directed anywhere.

This research has found that female language students displayed some predictable female speech patterns suggested by early feminist work but that such a display does not support a difference model. There are the problematics of gender identity that may be located in the negotiation of linguistic space. It was the teaching methods which revealed a strong gender bias in this classroom and provided evidence that gender construction is not only implicit but can also be explicit and spoken into existence in an ESL classroom.

Reflecting upon the grand debates surrounding girls' use of language leads me to the following speculations. Although examination of gendered speech strategies suggests a gender bias at the onset, the realities at work in this classroom do suggest these speech strategies may be helpful in indicating an emerging gendered identity. Gender is used as a filter for understanding this young ESL student: Zara is a female ESL student who is quiet but is also, importantly, silenced. She is ignored several times throughout the year in her attempts to speak, both by her teacher and by her classmates. The teacher appears to view her as a weak student and she says so herself. In primary ESL classrooms then, it would seem fair to suggest that gender can be a significant variable influencing expectations of behavior and, as such, should be carefully examined as possibly problematic in ESL environments. Also, clearly not all of the ESL practices promoted in the literature as necessary for language learning are being used; they do not seem to have been often used in this language classroom.

The main finding of this study provides new evidence of how gender is a prime variable in the language classroom. Though this notion is not new, the findings in Zara's classroom suggest marginalization and a construction of silence. If debates about gender in the classroom are thought to be a thing of a 1970s past, ones largely settled in other sociological debates, then this study suggests the debate is not over. The experiences of these young language learners in Canada suggest the battle for linguistic space is far from resolved. With energies shifting elsewhere as many of the recent debates appear focused on male experiences and under-achievement, it may be that the voices of ESL girls are under more threat of being silenced. Gender is not simply a political debate, one located in a particular time, as a particular trend. A language teacher must give attention to the speech production of female ESL students and give attention to both language teaching practices as well as to the attitudes which surround the classroom and govern the use of linguistic space.

Recommendations

It is important to recognize that some students (often girls) get little access to the linguistic space and do not protest, while others (often boys) are given opportunities to talk in classrooms by the teacher and the teaching methods. Clearly, classrooms are not benign, neutral sites: they are sites of linguistic struggle and the teacher can be a powerful force in governing participation. It is crucial that the language classroom and the language teacher be organized in such a way that gender is recognized as a serious variable in speech production. How this can be carried out is by no means simple because classroom day-to-day conversations are spontaneous and appear intuitive and natural. To shift linguistic space so as to provide ESL girls with more time to produce language will take more than awareness on the part of ESL educators: it will take strategy. My recommendations are directed to the ESL classrooms and to ESL teachers who wish to be better informed about the role of gender in an ESL setting and, as such, see speech production as a central part of learning a language. If girls speak less, will they learn less English and will their opportunities to think and communicate in complex ways be reduced? This may be likely.

It is vital that ESL teachers look at the way girls talk in their language classrooms. Examining the way girls use female speech strategies may bring about a degree of consciousness about their own interactions and their own perceptions of gender assumptions. More significantly, girls themselves may be able to understand that it is not just the 'watching' of English that may be important to learning English but the ways of speaking that impact upon relationships which lead to language development. Relationships in classrooms are central to producing language.

Particularly when girls are in class discussions, ESL teachers need to be aware of the extra pressures on female students, realizing that relationships are complex and that the linguistic space may be disproportionately allocated. Giving attention to girls who are speaking and to what they are saying will go a long way in supporting and validating a language learner. Waiting longer for replies or specifically asking girls to participate in conversations are not methods used in all language classrooms. These ESL teacher practices must be taught in teacher education programs. Even in primary language classrooms, gender is a powerful variable and primary teachers in particular must also admit this and govern their language classrooms with this in mind.

Finally it would appear appropriate for language teachers to structure talk related activities and to prepare girls for classroom discussions before they begin. It may be the case that teachers use talk as a preliminary activity yet often talk the entire lesson in an attempt to govern the learning, rather than permit linguistic space for language use and learning. However, it needs to be recognized that speech itself can determine learning opportunities and if girls are kept quiet, this silencing does great damage to their language learning potential. The argument that ESL girls may be shy and quiet of their own accord is irrelevant (as well as unsubstantiated) for it is the systematic silencing of girls that may need further attention. Such research needs to continue if we are to address the processes in ESL classrooms that limit the potential of silent students. 'Who is talking?' is a critical question for the ESL teacher. The stereotyping of Punjabi girls as quiet is simply not an adequate response to such enquiry. The realities of one ESL classroom suggest a more complex picture.

Last thoughts

I have hoped to show the powerful role of teaching methods in a language classroom, specifically concerning gender as a significant learner variable. In the relationship between Zara and Mrs. Smith, the teacher appeared at times to limit Zara by 'sh-shushing' her. She may have limited Zara's language acquisition by denying her linguistic space. However, Zara also participated in her own silence by remaining quiet. This case is just one particular case and is dependent on local understandings. But such local complexity implicates all ESL classrooms, each filled with unique issues. What all ESL classrooms share with this classroom is the variable of gender and its power in influencing speech acts. Such recognition of gender challenges our accepted ways of thinking about primary language classrooms as benign or neutral. They are not. This study invites an exploration of gender binaries and suggests a need to examine gender construction in language classrooms. In addition, I hope the study will bring awareness of the ongoing positioning of female speakers. Sometimes girls are not permitted linguistic space in their own language-learning classrooms. Finding ways for teachers and researchers to engage in dialogue concerning the impact of gender in the amount of speech production will be crucial in the field of second language acquisition. This study is offered as one contribution to such dialogue.

Finally, I urge language teachers to find ways to negotiate gender in their classrooms. Teachers can be aware that children are sensitive to the question of belonging and would do well to take measures to ensure that all students, including girls, are claiming and using linguistic space that ensures their participation and, therefore, their legitimate inclusion.

Bibliography

AAUWEF, American Association of University Women Educational Foundation and the Wellesley College Centre for Research on Women. (1992). *How schools shortchange girls.* Washington, DC: AAUW Educational Foundation.

Abella, R. (1991). Equality and human rights in Canada: Coping with the new isms. *University Affairs,* June/July: 21–22.

Acker, S. (1994). *Gendered education.* Buckingham: Open University Press.

Adelman, C. (Ed.) (1981). *Uttering, muttering: Collecting, using and reporting talk for social and educational research.* London: Grant McIntyre.

Alexander, M. (1996). *The shock of arrival: reflections on postcolonial experience.* Boston: South End Press.

Altani, C. (1995). Primary school teachers' explanations of boys' disruptiveness in the classroom: A gender-specific aspect of the hidden curriculum. In: S. Mills (Ed.), *Language and gender: Interdisciplinary perspectives.* Harlow, Essex: Addison Wesley Longman.

Angelo, M. (1997). *The Sikh diaspora: Tradition and change in an immigrant community.* New York: Garland Publishing.

Annau, C. (1999). *Just watch me,* Short Film. Toronto: National Film Board of Canada.

Anyon, J. (1983). Intersections of gender and class: Accommodation and resistance by working-class and affluent females to contradictory sex-role ideologies. In: S. Walker and L. Barton (Eds.), *Gender, class and education.* New York: Falmer Press.

Aries, E. (1997). Women and men talking: Are they worlds apart? In: M. R. Walsh (Ed.), *Women, men and gender.* London: Yale University Press.

Ashworth, M. (1992). Projecting the past into the future: A look at ESL for children in Canada. In: K. A. Moodley (Ed.), *Beyond multicultural education: International perspectives.* Calgary: Detselig.

Askew, S. and Ross, C. (1988). *Boys don't cry: Boys and sexism in education.* Milton Keyes: Open University Press.

Atkinson, P. and Hammersley, M. (1998). Ethnography and participant observation. In: N. K. Denzin and Y. S. Lincoln (Eds.), *Strategies of qualitative inquiry.* London: Sage.

Bailey, K. (1993). *The girls are the ones with the pointy nails.* London, Ontario: Althouse Press.

Bakhtin, M. M. (1996). The dialogic imagination: Four essays. In: M. Holquist (Ed.); trans. by Caryl Emerson and Michael Holquist. Austin, Texas: University of Texas Press.

Bannerji, H. (1993). Popular images of South Asian women. In: H. Bannerji (Ed.), *Returning the gaze: Essays on racism, feminism, and politics.* (pp. 176–186). Toronto: Sister Vision Press.

Bannerji, H. (2000). The paradox of diversity: The construction of a multicultural Canada and 'women of colour'. *Women's Studies International Forum,* 23 (5), 537–560.

Baumann, G. (1996). *Contesting culture: Discourses of identity in multi-ethnic London.* Cambridge: Cambridge University Press.

Baxter, J. (1999). Teaching girls to speak out: The female voice in public contexts. *Language and Education*, 13 (2), 81–98.

Baxter, J. (2002a). Jokers in the pack: Why boys are more adept than girls at speaking in public. *Language and Education*, 16 (2), 81–96.

Baxter, J. (2002b). A juggling act: A feminist post-structuralist analysis of girls' and boys' talk in the secondary classroom. *Gender and Education*, 14 (1), 5–19.

Baxter, J. (2003). *Positioning discourse in gender: A feminist methodology.* Basingstoke: Palgrave Macmillan.

Bell, D., Caplan, P. and Karim, W. (1993). *Gendered fields: Women, men and ethnography.* London: Routledge.

Bell, J. (1997). Teacher research in second and foreign language education. *The Canadian Modern Language Review*, 54, 3–10.

BERA Report. (2001). The Hay/McBer research into teacher effectiveness. *Research Intelligence* (BERA Newsletter) Number 75, 4–8.

Bergvall, V. L., Bing, J. M. and Freed, A. F. (1996). *Rethinking language and gender research.* New York: Addison Wesley Longman.

Berry, J. W. (1991). *Costs and benefits of multiculturalism: A psychological analysis.* Paper presented at the Canadian Studies Conference, St. John's College, University of Manitoba, Winnipeg, February 28–March 2.

Bhatti, G. (1995). A journey into the unknown: An ethnographic study of Asian children. In: M. Griffiths and B. Troyna (Eds.), *Antiracism, culture and social justice in education.* Stoke-on Trent, UK: Trentham Books.

Bhopal, K. (1997). *Gender, 'race' and patriarchy: A study of South Asian women.* Aldershot, England: Ashgate Publishing.

Biggs, A. and Edwards, V. (1991). 'I treat them all the same': Teacher–pupil talk in multi-ethnic classrooms. *Language and Education*, 5, 161–176.

Bissoondath, N. (1994). *Selling illusions. The cult of multiculturalism in Canada.* Toronto: Penguin Books.

Blair, M., Holland, J. and Sheldon, S. (Eds.) (1995). *Identity and diversity: Gender and the experience of education.* Clevedon: Multilingual Matters.

Bolan, K. (1999, 2000, 2001). Special correspondent Punjabi affairs. *The Vancouver Sun.* www.vancouversun.com

Bourdieu, P. (1992). *Language and symbolic power.* Cambridge: Polity.

Bourdieu, P. (2001). *Masculine domination.* Stanford, CA: Stanford University Press.

Bradley, J. (1998). Yanyuwa: 'Men speak one way, women speak another.' In: J. Coates (Ed.), *Language and gender: A reader.* (pp. 13–20). Oxford: Blackwell.

Brah, A. (1987). Women of South Asian origin in Britain: Issues and concerns. *South Asia Research*, 1, 1, 39–54.

Brah, A. and Minhas, R. (1985). Structural racism or cultural difference: Schooling for Asian girls. In: G. Weiner (Ed.), *Just a bunch of girls: Feminist approaches to schooling.* (pp. 14–25). Milton Keyes: Open University Press.

Buber, M. (1958). *I and thou.* Edinburgh: T and T Clark.

Bulbeck, C. (1998). *Re-orienting western feminisms.* Cambridge: Cambridge University Press.

Burgess, R. G. (Ed.) (1985). *Issues in educational research: Qualitative methods.* London: The Falmer Press.

Burn, E. (1989). Inside the Lego House. In: G. Weiner (Ed.), *Whatever happens to little women? Gender and primary schooling*. (pp. 139–148). Milton Keyes: Open University Press.

Burnet, J. (1984). Myths and multiculturalism. In: R. L. Samuda, J. W. Berry, M. Laferriere (Eds.), *Multiculturalism in Canada: Social and education perspectives*. (pp. 18–29). Toronto: Allyn and Bacon.

Burnet, J. and Palmer, H. (1988). *Coming Canadians: An introduction to the history of Canada's people*. Toronto: McClelland and Stewart.

Cameron, D. (1992). *Feminism and linguistic theory* (2nd ed.). New York: St. Martin's Press.

Cameron, D. (1995a). *Verbal hygiene*. London: Routledge.

Cameron, D. (1995b). Rethinking language and gender studies: Some issues for the 1990's. In: S. Mills (Ed.), *Language and gender: Interdisciplinary studies*. (pp. 31–44). London: Longman.

Cameron, D. (Ed.) (1998). *The feminist critique of language: A reader* (2nd ed.). London: Routledge.

Cameron, D. (2001). *Working with discourse*. London: Sage.

Canada. (1970). The royal commission on bilingualism and biculturalism. *Report: Volume IV. The contributions of other ethnic groups*. Ottawa: Queen's Printer.

Canada. (1971). House of Commons. *Debates 8*: 8545–48. October 8.

Canada. (1988). An Act for the preservation and enhancement of multiculturalism in Canada (Bill c-93). House of Commons.

Canadian Human Rights Foundation. (1987). *Multiculturalism and the charter*. Toronto: Carswell.

Carspecken, P. F. (1996). *Critical ethnography in educational research*. New York: Routledge.

Carter, K. and Stitzack, C. (Eds.) (1989). *Doing research on women's communication: Perspectives on theory and method*. Norwood, NJ: Ablex.

Cazden, C. (1988). *Classroom discourse: The language of teaching and learning*. Portsmouth, NH: Heinemann.

Celce-Murcia, M. (1987). Teaching pronunciation as communication. In: J. Morley (Ed.), *Current perspectives on pronunciation: Practices anchored in theory*. (pp. 5–12). Washington, DC: TESOL.

Charles, C. M. (1995). *Introduction to educational research* (2nd ed.). White Plains, NY: Longman.

Chaudron, C. (1988). *Second language classroom: Research on teaching and learning*. Cambridge: Cambridge University Press.

Cheshire, J. (1998). Linguistic variation and social function. In: J. Coates (Ed.), *Language and gender: A reader*. (pp. 29–41). Oxford: Blackwell.

Cheshire, J., Graddol, D. and Swann, J. (1987). *Describing language*. Milton Keynes: Open University Press.

Chomsky, N. (1968). *Language and mind*. New York: Harcourt, Brace and World.

Clark, A. and Trafford, J. (1996). Return to gender: Boys' and girls' attitudes and achievements. *Language Learning Journal*, 14, 40–49.

Clarricoates, K. (1978). Dinosaurs in the classroom: An examination of some of the aspects of the hidden curriculum in primary schools. *Women's Studies International Quarterly*, 1, 353–364.

Coates, J. (1993). *Women, men, and language: A sociolinguistic account of gender differences in language* (2nd ed.). London: Longman.

Coates, J. (1996). *Women talk: Conversations between women friends*. Oxford: Blackwell.

Coates, J. (1998a). Introduction. In: J. Coates (Ed.), *Language and gender: A reader*. (pp. 1–5). Oxford: Blackwell.

Coates, J. (1998b). 'Thank God I'm a woman': The construction of differing femininities. In: D. Cameron (Ed.), *The feminist critique of language: A reader* (2nd ed.). (pp. 295–322). London: Routledge.

Cochran, E. P. (1996). Gender and the ESL classroom. *TESOL Quarterly*, 30, 159–162.

Cohen, A. D. (1980). *Testing language ability in the classroom*. New York: Newbury House.

Cohen, A. D. (1984). On taking language tests: What the students report. *Language Testing*, 1 (1), 70–81.

Cohen, A. D. (1987). Student processing of feedback on their compositions. In: A. L. Wenden and J. Rubin (Eds.), *Learner strategies in language learning*. (pp. 57–69). Englewood Cliffs, NJ: Prentice-Hall International.

Cole, W. O. and Sambhi, P. S. (1978). *The Sikhs*. London: Routledge and Kegan Paul.

Cole, W. O. and Sambhi, P. S. (1990). *A popular dictionary of Sikhism*. Chicago: NTC Publishing Group.

Connell, R. W. (1995). *Masculinities*. Cambridge: Polity Press.

Connell, R. W., Ashendon, D. J., Kessler, S. and Dowsett, G. W. (1982). *Making the difference: Schools, families, and social diversion*. Sydney: George Allen and Unwin.

Connolly, P. (1995). Boys will be boys?: Racism, sexuality and the construction of masculine identities amongst infant boys. In: J. Holland, M. Blair and S. Sheldon (Eds.), *Debates and issues in feminist research and pedagogy*. Clevedon, UK: Multilingual Matters.

Cooke, S. (1998). *Collaborative learning activities in the classroom*. Leicester: Resource Centre for Multicultural Education.

Corson, D. (1993). *Language, minority education and gender: Linking social justice and power*. Clevedon: Multilingual Matters, Ltd.

Coulthard, M. (1985). *An introduction to discourse analysis*. London: Longman.

Crawford, M. (1995). *Talking difference: On gender and language*. London: Sage.

Crossley, N. (1996). *Intersubjectivity: The fabric of social becoming*. London: Sage.

Cumming, A. and Gill, J. (1992). Motivation or accessibility? Factors permitting Indo-Canadian women to pursue ESL literacy instruction. In: B. Burnaby and A. Cumming (Eds.), *Socio-political aspects of ESL*. Toronto: OISE Press.

Cummins, J. (Ed.) (1983). *Heritage language education: Issues and directions*. Ottawa: Ministry of Supply Services.

Cummins, J. (1985). Language and Canadian multiculturalism: Research and politics. In: M. R. Lupul (Ed.), *Osvita: Ukrainian bilingual education*. Edmonton: Canadian Institute of Ukrainian Studies, University of Alberta Press.

Cummins, J. (1993). The research basis for heritage language promotion. In: M. Danesi, K. McLeod and S. Morris (Eds.), *Heritage languages and education: The Canadian experience*. (pp. 1–22). Oakville: Mosaic Press.

Cummins, J. (1996). *Negotiating identities: Education for empowerment in a diverse society*. Ontario: CABE.

Cummins, J. and Danesi, M. (1990). *Heritage languages: The development and denial of Canada's linguistic resources*. Montreal: Our Schools/Our Selves Education Foundation.

Cummins, J. and Swain, M. (1986). *Bilingualism in education*. New York: Longman.

Davies, B. (1993). *Shards of glass: Children reading and writing beyond gendered identities*. Cresskill, NJ: Hampton Press.

Davies, C. A. (1991). *Reflexive ethnography*. London: Routledge.

Davies, J. (1999). *Expressions of gender: An enquiry into the way gender impacts on the discourse styles of pupils involved in small group talk during GCSE English lessons with particular reference to the under-achievement of boys*. Unpublished doctoral thesis. University of Sheffield.

Day, E. (1999). *Identity formation in a kindergarten English language learner: An ethnographic case study*. Unpublished doctoral thesis. Simon Fraser University, Burnaby, BC, Canada.

Deh, E. (1986). Women as object: The feminine condition in a decadent patriarchy. In: C. D. Narasimhaiah (Ed.), *Women in fiction and fiction by women: The Indian scene*. (pp. 9–19). India: Dhvanyaloka Press.

deHouwer, A. (1990). *The acquisition of two languages from birth: A case study*. Cambridge: Cambridge University Press.

Delamont, S. (1980). *The sociology of women*. London: George Allen and Unwin.

Delamont, S. (1990). *Sex roles and the school* (2nd ed.). London: Routledge.

Delamont, S. and Atkinson, P. (1995). *Fighting familiarity: Essays on education and ethnography*. Cresskill, NJ: Hampton Press.

Delpit, L. (1988). The silenced dialogue: Power and pedagogy in educating other people's children. *Harvard Educational Review*, 58 (3), 280–298.

Derrick, J. (1977). *Language needs of minority group children: Learners of English as a second language*. Windsor: NFER Publishing.

Descartes, R. (1969). *Discourse on method and the meditations*. Harmondsworth: Penguin.

Dewey, J. (1938). *Experience and education*. New York: Macmillan.

Diller, A., Houston, B., Morgan, K. P. and Ayim, M. (1996). *The gender question in education. Theory, pedagogy, and politics*. Oxford: Westview Press.

Driscoll, K. and McFarland, J. (1989). The impact of a feminist perspective on research methodologies: Social sciences. In: W. Tomm (Ed.), *The effects of feminist approaches on research methodologies*. Waterloo: Wilfrid Laurier University Press.

Drudy, S. and Chathain, M. U. (1999). *Gender equality in classroom interaction*. Co. Kildare: National University of Ireland.

Dubin, F. and Olshtain, E. (1977). *Facilitating language learning: A guidebook for the ESL/EFL teacher*. New York: McGraw-Hill.

Dubin, F. and Olshtain, E. (1986). *Course design: Developing programs and materials for language learning*. New York: Cambridge University Press.

Dubin, F. and Olshtain, E. (1987). *Let's stop putting vocabulary under the rug*. Paper presented at the 21st Annual TESOL Convention, Miami, FL.

Dubin, F. and Olshtain, E. (1990). *Reading by all means*. Reading, MA: Addison-Wesley.

Dulay, H., Burt, M. and Krashen, S. D. (1982). *Language two*. Oxford: Oxford University Press.

Eckert, P. (1989). Gender and sociolinguistic variation. In: J. Coates (Ed.), *Language and gender: A reader.* (pp. 64–75). Oxford: Blackwell.

Eckert, P. (1990). The whole woman: Sex and gender differences in variation. *Language variation and change.* 1: 245–67.

Eckert, P. and McConnell-Ginet, S. (1992). Think practically and look locally: Language and gender as community-based practice. *Annual Review of Anthropology.* 21: 461–90.

Edelsky, G. (1981). Who's got the floor? *Language in Society,* 10, 383–421.

Edwards, V. and Redfern, A. (1992). *The world in a classroom: Language in education in Britain and Canada.* Clevedon, UK: Multilingual Matters.

Eggins, S. and Slade, D. (1997). *Analysing casual conversation.* London: Cassell.

Ehrlich, S. (1997). Gender as social practice: Implications for second language acquisition. *Studies in Second Language Acquisition,* 19, 421–446.

Eisikovitz, E. (1998). Girl-talk/boy-talk: Sex differences in adolescent speech. In: J. Coates (Ed.), *Language and gender: A reader.* (pp. 42–53). Oxford: Blackwell.

Elbow, P. (1973). *Writing without teachers.* New York: Oxford University Press.

Elbow, P. (1985). The challenge for sentence combining. In: D. Daiker, A. Kerek and M. Morenberg (Eds.), *Sentence combining: A rhetorical perspective.* (pp. 232–245). Carbondale, IL: Southern Illinois University Press.

Epstein, D., Elwood, J., Hey, V. and Maw, J. (Eds.) (1998). *Failing boys? Issues in gender and achievement.* Buckingham: Open University Press.

Evans, T. (1988). *A gender agenda: A sociological study of teachers, parents and pupils in their primary schools.* Sydney: Allen and Unwin Australia.

Fairclough, N. (1989). *Language and power.* London: Longman.

Fairclough, N. (1995). *Critical discourse analysis: The critical study of language.* London: Longman.

Faludi, S. (1993). *Backlash: The undeclared war against women.* New York: Vintage.

Fetterman, P. M. (1989). *Ethnography: Step by step.* London: Sage.

Fisher, H. (1999). *The first sex.* New York: Ballentine Books.

Fishman, J. (1989). *Language and ethnicity in minority sociolinguistic matters.* Clevedon, UK: Multilingual Matters.

Fishman, P. (1983). Interaction: The work women do. In: B. Thorne and N. Henley (Eds.), *Language, gender and society.* (pp. 89–101). Rowley, Mass: Newbury House.

Fitzpatrick, F. (1987). *The open door.* Avon: Multilingual Matters.

Flanders, N. (1970). *Analyzing teacher behavior.* London: Addison-Wesley.

Fleras, A. and Elliott, J. (1992). *Multiculturalism in Canada.* Scarborough, ON: Nelson Canada.

Flyvbjerb, B. (2001). *Making social science matter.* Cambridge: Cambridge University Press.

Gabriel, S. L. and Smithson, I. (Eds.) (1990). *Gender in the classroom: Power and pedagogy.* Urbana: University of Illinois Press.

Gal, S. (1991). Between speech and silence: the problematics of research on language and gender. *Papers in Pragmatics,* 3 (1), 1–38.

Gallas, K. (1998). *'Sometimes I can be anything': Power, gender in a primary classroom.* New York: Teachers College Press.

Gambell, T. and Hunter, D. (2000). Surveying gender differences in Canadian school literacy. *Journal of Curriculum Studies,* 32 (5), 689–719.

Geertz, C. (1973). *The interpretation of cultures: Selected essays.* New York: Basic Books.

George, R. and Maguire, M. (1998). Older women training to teach. *Gender and Education,* 10 (4), 417–430.

Ghosh, R. (1996). *Redefining multicultural education.* Toronto: Harcourt Brace and Co.

Ghuman, P. A. S. (1994). *Coping with two cultures: British Asian and Indo-Canadian adolescents.* Clevedon, UK: Multilingual Matters.

Gibbon, M. (1999). *Feminist perspectives on language.* London: Longman.

Gibbons, P. (1998). *Learning to learn in a second language.* Marrickville, NSW: Southwood Press.

Gibson, M. A. (1988). *Accommodation without assimilation: Sikh immigrants in an American high school.* Ithaca: Cornell University Press.

Gilbert, P. and Taylor, S. (1991). *Fashioning the feminine.* North Sydney, Australia: Allen and Unwin.

Gilligan, C. (1982/1992). *In a different voice: Psychological theory and women's development.* Cambridge, MA: Harvard University Press.

Globe and Mail. (2000). www.globeandmail.com. Keyword: Punjabi.

Goldberger, N. (1997). Ways of knowing: Does gender matter? In: M. R. Walsh (Ed.), *Women, men, and gender.* (pp. 252–260). London: Yale University Press.

Goodwin, M. H. (1990). *He-said-she-said.* Bloomington: Indiana University Press.

Graddol, P. and Swann, J. (1989). *Gender voices.* Oxford: Blackwell.

Graham, S. and Rees, F. (1995). Gender differences in language learning: The question of control. *Language Learning Journal,* (11), 18–19.

Gray, J. (2002). *Men are from Mars, women are from Venus: A practical guide for improving communication and getting what you want.* New York: Harper Collins.

Grossberg, L. (1993). Cultural studies and/in new worlds. In: McCarthy and W. Crichlow (Eds.), *Race, identity, and representation in education.* (pp. 89–108). London: Routledge.

Gumperz, J. J. (1982). *Discourse strategies.* New York: Cambridge University Press.

Gupta, S. and Umar, A. (1994). Barriers to achievement faced by immigrant women of colour. In: J. Gallivan, S. D. Crozier and V. M. Lalande (Eds.), *Women, girls, and achievement.* (pp. 56–62). North York: Captus University Press.

Habermas, J. (1987). *The theory of communicative action. Vol. Two: System and Lifeworld.* Cambridge: Polity.

Hall, K. and Bucholtz, M. (Eds.) (1995). *Gender articulated: Language and the socially constructed self.* New York: Routledge.

Hall, S. (1992). Cultural identity and diaspora. *Framework,* 36, 222–237.

Hall, S. (1996). Introduction: Who needs identity? In: S. Hall and P. duGay (Eds.), *Questions of cultural identity.* (pp. 1–17). London: Sage.

Hammersley, M. (1992). *What's wrong with ethnography.* London: Routledge.

Hammersley, M. (1998). *Reading ethnographic research: A critical guide* (2nd ed.). Essex: Addison Wesley Longman.

Hammersley, M. (2000). The relevance of qualitative research. *Oxford Review of Education,* 26, 3 and 4, 393–405.

Hammersley, M. and Atkinson, P. (1983). *Ethnography: Principles and practice.* New York: Tavistock.

Haverson, W. W. (1986). Adult illiteracy: Implications for parent involvement. In: *Issues of parent involvement and literacy.* Washington, DC: Trinity College.

Haverson, W. W. and Haynes, J. (1982). *Literacy training for ESL adult learners*. Washington, DC: Centre for Applied Linguistics.

Haw, K. (1998). *Educating Muslim girls: Shifting discourse*. Buckingham: Open University Press.

Herberg, E. N. (1989). *Ethnic groups in Canada: Adaptations and transitions*. Scarborough: Nelson Canada.

Hey, V. (1997). *The company she keeps: An ethnography of girls' friendship*. Buckingham, UK: Open University Press.

Holmes, J. (1991). State of the art: Language and gender. *Language Teaching*. October 1991: Special feature. 207–219.

Holmes, J. (1992). *An introduction to sociolinguistics*. New York: Longman.

Holmes, J. (1994). Improving the lot of female language learners. In: J. Sunderland (Ed.), *Exploring gender*. (pp. 156–162). London: Prentice Hall.

Holmes, J. (1995). *Women, men and politeness*. Harlow, Essex: Addison Wesley Longman.

Holmes, J. (1998). Women's talk: The question of sociolinguistic universals. In: J. Coates (Ed.), *Language and gender: A reader*. (pp. 461–483). Oxford: Blackwell.

Hull, G. T., Bell-Scott, P. and Smith, P. (Eds.) (1982). *All the women are white, all the blacks are men, and some of us are brave*. Old Westbury, NY: The Feminist Press.

Hymes, D. (1972). Introduction. In: C. B. Cazden, V. P. John and D. Hymes (Eds.), *Functions of language in the classroom*. (pp. xi–lvii). New York: Teachers College Press.

Irvine, J. M. (1995). *Sexuality education across cultures: Working with differences*. San Francisco: Jossey-Bass Publishers.

Iwataki, S. (1981). Preparing to teach adult education programs. In: J. C. Fisher, M. A. Clark and J. Schachter (Eds.), On TESOL 80: Building bridges: Research and practice in teaching ESL. (pp. 23–24). Washington, DC: TESOL.

Jagpal, S. S. (1994). *Becoming Canadians: Pioneer Sikhs in their own words*. Vancouver: Harbour Publishing.

Jaworski, A. (1993). *The power of silence*. London: Sage.

Jay, G. (1995). Taking multiculturalism personally: Ethnos and ethos in the classroom. In: Jane Gallop (Ed.), *Pedagogy: The question of impersonation*. (pp. 117–128). Bloomington: Indiana University Press.

Johnston, H. (1984). *The East Indians in Canada*. Ottawa: Canadian Historical Association.

Johnston, H. (1989). *The voyage of the Komagata Maru: The Sikh challenge to Canada's colour bar*. (2nd ed.). Vancouver: UBC Press.

Jones, C. and Maguire, M. (1998). Needed and wanted? The school experiences of some minority ethnic trainee teachers in the UK. *European Journal of Intercultural Studies*, 9 (1), 79–92.

Jones, C. and Mahony, P. (Eds.) (1989). *Learning our lines: Sexuality and social control in education*. London: Women's Press.

Jones, D. (1980). Gossip: Notes on women's oral culture. In: C. Kramarae (Ed.), *The voices and words of women and men*. (pp. 193–198). Oxford: Pergamon Press.

Jones, M., Kitetu, C. and Sunderland, J. (1997). Discourse roles, gender and language textbook dialogues: Who learns what from John and Sally? *Gender and Education*, 9 (4), 469–490.

Julé, A. (2001). Speaking her sex: Gender in an ESL classroom. Paper presented at BAAL Conference, University of Reading, Reading, UK. September 6–8.

Julé, A. (2002). Speaking their sex. A study of gender and linguistic space in an ESL classroom. *TESL Canada Journal,* 19, 2 (Spring), 37–51.

Julé, A. (2003a). Linguistic space: An ethnographic study of gender in an ESL classroom. In G. Walford (Ed.), *Investigating educational policy through ethnography.* (pp. 215–230). Oxford: Elsevier Science.

Julé, A. (2003b). Speaking in silence: A case study. In TESOL Special Edition. In: B. Norton and A. Paulenko. (Eds.), *Gender and TESOL.* Harvard: TESOL Press.

Kapur, R. (1986). *Sikh separatism: The politics of faith.* London: Allen and Unwin.

Kothandaraman, B. (1992). The child is the mother of the woman: Girl children in T.V. ads. In: V. Kirpal (Ed.), *The girl child in 20th century Indian literature.* (pp. 38–43). New Delhi: Sterling Publishers.

Kramarae, C. (1984). Introduction: Toward an understanding of language and power. In: C. Kramaral et al. (Eds.), *Language and power.* (pp. 9–22). Beverly Hills: Sage.

Kramsch, C. (1993). *Context and culture in language teaching.* Oxford: Oxford University Press.

Krashen, S. D. (1982, 1995). *Principles and practice in second language acquisition.* Oxford: Pergamon Press.

Krashen, S. D. and Terrell, T. D. (1983). *The natural approach: Language acquisition in the classroom.* Oxford: Pergamon Press.

Kroll, B. (1990). The rhetoric/syntax split: Designing a curriculum for ESL students. *Journal of Basic Writing,* 9 (1), 40–55.

Kutnick, P. (1988). *Relationships in the primary school classroom.* London: Paul Chapman Publishing.

Labov, W. (1970). The study of language in its social context. In: P. Giglioli (Ed.). (1972), *Language and social context.* (pp. 253–283). Middlesex: Penguin.

Lacan, J. (1968). *The language of the self: The function of language in psychoanalysis.* (trans. Anthony Wilden). Baltimore: John Hopkins University Press.

Lakoff, R. (1975). *Language and woman's place.* New York, NY: Harper and Row.

Lakoff, R. (1995). Cries and whispers: The shattering of the silence. In: K. Hall and M. Bucholtz (Eds.), *Gender articulated: Language and the socially constructed self.* (pp. 25–50). London: Routledge.

Lambert, R. D. and Curtis, J. (1989). The racial attitudes of Canadians. In: L. Tepperman and J. Curtis (Eds.), *Readings in sociology.* (pp. 343–348). Toronto: McGraw-Hill Ryerson.

Larsen-Freeman, D. and Long, M. H. (1991). *An introduction to second language acquisition research.* New York: Longman.

Lather, P. (1991). *Getting smart: Feminist research and pedagogy with/in the postmodern.* New York: Routledge.

Lave, J. (1988). *Cognition in practice: Mind, mathematics and culture in everyday life.* Cambridge: Cambridge University Press.

Lave, J. and Wenger, E. (1991). *Situated learning: Legitimate peripheral participation.* Cambridge: Cambridge University Press.

Lee, A. (1996). *Gender, literacy, curriculum: Re-writing school geography.* London: Taylor and Francis.

Leki, I. (1990). Coaching from the margins: Issues in written response. In B. Kroll (Ed.), *Second language writing: Research insights for the classroom.* New York: Cambridge University Press.

Lloyd, B. and Duveen, G. (1992). *Gender identities and education: The impact of starting school.* Exeter: St. Martin's Press.

Luke, C. and Gore, J. (Eds.) (1992). *Feminisms and critical pedagogy.* New York: Routledge.

Mac an Ghaill, M. (2000). The cultural production of English masculinities in late modernity. *Canadian Journal of Education,* 25 (2), 88–101.

MacNamee and White. (1985). Heritage language in preschool. *Language and Society,* 15, 20–23.

McAndrew, M. (1987). Ethnicity, multiculturalism, and multicultural education in Canada. In: R. Ghosh and D. Ray (Eds.), *Diversity and unity in education: A comparative analysis.* (pp. 143–154). London: George Allen and Unwin.

McBer, H. (2000). A model of teacher effectiveness report to the Department for Education and Employment (DfEE). On-line. http://www.dfee.gov.uk/teaching reforms/leadership/mcber/02.shtml.

McLeod, K. (1993). Bilingualism, multilingualism, and multiculturalism: A retrospective of western Canada since the 1870s. In M. Danesi, K. McLeod and S. Morris. (Eds.), *Heritage languages and education: The Canadian experience.* (pp. 33–52). Oakville: Mosaic Press.

McLeod, W. H. (1984). *Textual sources for the study of Sikhism.* New Jersey: Barnes and Noble Books.

McLeod, W. H. (1989a). *The Sikhs: History, religion and society.* New York: Columbia University Press.

McLeod, W. H. (1989b). *Who is a Sikh: The problem of Sikh identity.* Oxford: Oxford University Press.

Maguire, M. (1993). Women who teach teachers. *Gender and Education,* 5 (3), 269–281.

Maguire, M. (1997). Missing links: Working-class women of Irish descent. In: P. Mahony and C. Zmroczek (Eds.), *Class matters: 'Working-class' women's perspectives on social class.* (pp. 87–100). London: Taylor and Francis, Inc.

Mahony, P. (1985). *Schools for the boys?: Co-education reassessed.* London: Hutchinson.

Mahony, P. (1998). Girls will be girls and boys will be first. In: D. Epstein, J. Ellwood, V. Hey and J. Maw (Eds.), *Failing boys? Issues in gender and achievement.* (pp. 37–56). Buckingham: Open University Press.

Mahony, P. and Hextall, I. (2000). *Reconstructing teaching: Standards, performance and accountability.* London: Routledge Falmer.

May, S. (1999). Introduction: Towards critical multiculturalism. In S. May (Ed.), *Critical Multiculturalism.* (pp. 1–10). London: Falmer.

May, S. (2001). *Language and minority rights: Ethnicity, nationalism, and the politics of language.* Harlow, Essex: Pearson Education.

Merleau-Ponty, M. (1962). *The phenomenology of perception.* London: Routledge.

Mertens, D. M. (1998). *Research methods in education and psychology.* London: Sage.

Miles, M. B. and Huberman, A. M. (1994). *Qualitative data analysis.* (2nd ed.). London: Sage.

Mills, S. (Ed.) (1995). *Language and gender: Interdisciplinary perspectives.* New York: Longman.

Minhas, M. S. (1994). *The Sikh Canadians.* Edmonton: Reidmore Books.

Moir, A. and Moir, B. (1998). *Why men don't iron.* London: Harper Collins.

Moll, L. C. (1992). Bilingual classroom studies and community analysis: Some recent trends. *Educational Researcher,* 21, 20–24.

Moodley, K. (1983). Canadian multiculturalism as ideology. *Ethnic and Racial Studies,* 6 (3), 320–332.

Moodley, K. (1999). Antiracist education through political literacy: The case of Canada. In S. May (Ed.), *Critical multiculturalism.* (pp. 138–152). London: Falmer.

Morrison, T. (1993). *Playing in the dark.* New York: Vintage Books.

Myers, K. (Ed.) (2000). *Whatever happened to equal opportunities in schools?* Buckingham: Open University Press.

Nabar, V. (1992). What little girls are made into: Socialisation of the girl child. In: V. Kirpal (Ed.), *The girl child in 20th century Indian literature.* (pp. 53–62). New Delhi: Sterling Publishers.

Nanda, S. (2000). *Gender diversity: Cross-cultural variations.* Prospect Heights, Ill: Waveland Press.

Ng, R. (1993). Racism, sexism, and nation building in Canada. In: C. McCarthy and W. Crichlow (Eds.), *Race identity and representation in education.* (pp. 50–59). New York: Routledge.

Nichols, P. (1983). Linguistic options and choices for women in the rural south. In: B. Thorne, C. Kramarae and N. Henley (Eds.), *Language, gender and society.* (pp. 54–68). Rowley MA: Newbury House.

Nichols, P. (1998). Black women in the rural south: Conservative and innovative. In: J. Coates (Ed.), *Language and gender: A reader.* (pp. 55–63). Oxford: Blackwell.

Norton, B. (1995). Social identity, investment, and language learning. *TESOL Quarterly,* 29 (1), 9–31.

Norton, B. (1997). Language, identity, and the ownership of English. *TESOL Quarterly,* 31, 409–429.

Norton, B. (2000). *Identity and language learning: Gender, ethnicity and educational change.* Essex: Pearson Education.

O'Barr, W. and Atkins, B. (1980). 'Women's language' or 'powerless language'? In: S. McConnell-Ginet, N. Furman and R. Borker (Eds.), *Women and language in literature and society.* (pp. 93–110). New York: Praeger.

Ochs, E. (1988). *Culture and language development: Language acquisition and language socialization in a Samoan village.* Cambridge: Cambridge University Press.

Orenstein, P. (1994). *School girls: Young women, self-esteem, and the confidence gap.* New York: Doubleday.

Oxford, R. (1993). Instructional implications of gender differences in a second/foreign language (L2) learning styles and strategies. *Applied Language Learning,* 4, (142).

Oxford, R. (1994). La différence ...: Gender differences in second/foreign language learning styles and strategies. In: J. Sunderland (Ed.), *Exploring gender: Questions and implications for English language education.* (pp. 140–147). New York: Prentice Hall.

Paechter, C. (1998). *Educating the other: Gender, power and schooling.* London: Falmer.

Paechter, C. and Head, J. (1996). Gender, identity, status and the body: Life in a marginal subject. *Gender and Education,* 8 (1), 21–29.

Pauwels, A. (1998). *Women changing language.* Harlow, Essex, UK: Addison-Wesley Longman.

Piaget, J. (1932). *The moral judgment of the child.* Glencoe, Ill: Free Press.

Pilkington, J. (1998). 'Don't try and make out that I'm nice': The different strategies women and men use when gossiping. In: J. Coates (Ed.), *Language and gender: A reader.* (pp. 254–269). Oxford: Blackwell.

Raj, S. C. (1991). *Understanding Sikhs and their religion.* Winnipeg: Kindred Press.

Rampton, B. (1991). Second language learners in a stratified multilingual setting. *Applied Linguistics,* 12 (3), 229–248.

Rampton, B. (1995). *Crossing: Language and ethnicity among adolescents.* London: Longman.

Rampton, B. (2000). Continuity and change in views of society in applied linguistics. *Change and continuity in applied linguistics, BAAL.* (pp. 97–114). Clevedon, UK: Multilingual Matters.

Rich, A. (1984). *On lies, secrets and silence: Selected prose 1966–1978.* London: Virago.

Robson, C. (1993). *Real world research: A resource for social scientists and practitioner-researchers.* Oxford: Blackwell.

Rogoff, B. (1994). Developing understanding of the idea of communities of learners. *Mind, Culture, and Activity,* 1 (4), 209–229.

Sadker, M. and Sadker, D. (1994). *Failing at fairness: How America's schools cheat girls.* New York: Scribner's.

Sapir, E. (1929). The status of linguistics as a science. In: E. Sapir (Ed.), *Selected writings in language, culture and personality* (1949). (pp. 160–166). Berkeley: California Press.

Searle, J. R. (1969). *Speech acts.* Cambridge: Cambridge University Press.

Shakespeare, W. *King Lear.* Hertfordshire: Wordsworth Classics (1994).

Shamaris, C. (1990). Deepa's story: Writing non-sexist stories for a reception class. In: E. Tutchell (Ed.), *Dolls and dungarees: Gender issues in the primary school curriculum.* (pp. 52–61). Milton Keynes: Open University Press.

Sharpe, S. (1976). *'Just like a girl': How girls learn to be women.* Middlesex: Penguin Books.

Sheldon, A. (1997). Talking power: Girls, gender enculturation and discourse. In: R. Wodak (Ed.), *Gender and discourse.* (pp. 225–244). London: Sage.

Short, G. and Carrington, B. (1989). Discourse on gender: The perceptions of children aged six and eleven. In: C. Skelton (Ed.), *Whatever happens to little women?: Gender and primary schooling.* Milton Keyes: Open University Press.

Siemens, A. H. (1990). The process of settlement in the Lower Fraser Valley in its provincial context. In: A. H. Siemens (Ed.), *Lower fraser valley: Evolution of a cultural landscape.* (pp. 27–49). Vancouver: Tantalus.

Singh, G. S. (1980). *The religion of the Sikh.* New York: Asia Publishing House.

Skelton, (Ed.) (1989). *Whatever happens to little women?* Milton Keynes: Open University Press.

Smith, J. (1987). Institutional ethnography: A feminist method. *Resources for Feminist Research/Documentation sur la recherché féministe,* 15, 6–13.

Soskin, W. and John, V. (1963). The study of spontaneous talk. In: R. Barker (Ed.), *The stream of behavior.* New York: Appleton-Century-Croft.

Spender, D. (1980a). *Man made language.* London: Routledge Kegan Paul.

Spender, D. (1980b). Talking in the class. In: Spender, D. and E. Sarah (Eds.), *Learning to lose: Sexism and education.* (pp. 148–154). London: The Women's Press.

Spender, D. (1982). *Invisible women: The schooling scandal*. London: Writers and Readers Publishing Corp.

Spender, D. and Sarah, E. (Eds.) (1980). *Learning to lose: Sexism and education*. London: The Women's Press.

Stake, R. E. (1995). *The art of case study research*. London: Sage.

Stanworth, M. (1981). *Gender and schooling: A study of sexual divisions in the classroom*. Explorations in Feminism No. 7. London: Women's Research and Resources Centre.

Statistics Canada 1999. Government of Canada. On-line: http://infocan.gc.ca/facts.

Steedman, C. (1985). 'Listen, how the caged bird sings': Amarjit's song. In: C. Steedman, C. Urwin and V. Walkerdine (Eds.), *Language, gender and childhood*. (pp. 137–163).

Steinberg, S. (1981). *The ethnic myth*. Boston: Beacon Press.

Stern, H. H. (1983). *Fundamental concepts of language teaching*. Oxford: Oxford University Press.

Stern, S. L. (1985). *Teaching literature in ESL/EFL: An integrated approach*. Dissertation Abstracts International, 46. (University Microfilms No. DER 85-13164).

Stokoe, E. (1997). An evaluation of two studies of gender and language in educational contexts: Some problems in analysis. *Gender and Education, 9* (2), 233–244.

Streitmatter, J. (1994). *Toward gender equality in the classroom: Everyday teacher's beliefs and practices*. Albany: State University of New York Press.

Stubbs, M. (1976). *Language, schools and classrooms*. London: Methuen and Co.

Sunderland, J. (Ed.) (1994). *Exploring gender: Questions and implications for English language education*. New York: Prentice Hall.

Sunderland, J. (1995). 'We're boys, miss!': Finding gendered identities and looking for gendering of identities in the foreign language classroom. In: S. Mills (Ed.), *Language and gender: Interdisciplinary perspectives*. (pp. 160–178). New York: Longman.

Sunderland, J. (1998). Girls being quiet: A problem for foreign language classrooms. *Language Teaching Research, 2*.

Swann, J. (1998). Talk control: An illustration from the classroom of problems in analysing male dominance of conversation. In: J. Coates (Ed.), *Language and gender: A reader*. (pp. 185–196). Oxford: Blackwell.

Swann, J. and Graddol, D. (1995). Feminising classroom talk? In: S. Mills (Ed.), *Language and gender: Interdisciplinary perspectives*. (pp. 135–148). Harlow, Essex: Addison Wesley Longman.

Swann, J. and Stubbs, M. (1992). *Girls, boys and language*. Oxford: Blackwell.

Szirom, T. (1988). *Teaching gender?: Sex education and sexual stereotypes*. Sydney: Allen and Unwin.

Talbot, M. (1998). *Language and gender: An introduction*. Cambridge: Blackwell.

Tannen, D. (1989a). *Talking voices: repetition, dialogue, and imagery in conversational discourse*. Cambridge: Cambridge University Press.

Tannen, D. (1989b). *Conversational style: Analyzing talk among friends*. Norwood, NJ: Ablex.

Tannen, D. (1990). *You just don't understand: Women and men in conversation*. New York: Ballentine Books.

Tannen, D. (1994). *Gender and discourse*. Oxford: Oxford University Press.

Tannen, D. (1995). *Talking from 9 to 5*. London: Virago.

Tannen, D. (1996). Researching gender-related patterns in classroom discourse. *TESOL Quarterly*, 30 (2), 341–344.

Tannen, D. (1997). Women and men talking: An interactional sociolinguistic approach. In: M. R. Walsh (Ed.), *Women, men, and gender: Ongoing debates*. (pp. 82–90). NewHaven: Yale University Press.

Tannen, D. (1998). *The argument culture*. London: Virago.

Taylor, C. (1992). *Multiculturalism and the politics of recognition*. Princeton, NJ: Princeton University Press.

Taylor, C. (1994). The politics of recognition. In: A. Gutman (Ed.), *Multiculturalism*. Princeton: Princeton University Press.

Taylor, T. J. and Cameron, D. (1987). *Analysing conversation: Rules and units in the structure of talk*. Oxford: Pergamon Press.

Thompson, B. (1989). Teacher attitudes: Complacency and conflict. In: G. Weiner (Ed.), *Whatever happens to little women? Gender and primary schooling*. (pp. 68–78). Milton Keyes: Open University Press.

Thompson, L. (Ed.) (1997). *Children talking: The development of pragmatic competence*. Clevedon: Multicultural Matters.

Thornborrow, J. (2002) *Power talk*. London: Longman.

Thornborrow, J. and Wareing, S. (1998). *Patterns in language: An introduction to language and literary style*. London: Routledge.

Thorne, B. (1993). *Gender play: Girls and boys in school*. Buckingham, UK: Open University Press.

Ting-Toomey, S. (1987). Introduction: The pragmatics of gender-related communication. In: L. P. Stewart and S. Ting-Toomey (Eds.), *Communication, gender, and sex roles in diverse interaction contexts*. New Jersey: Ablex.

Tolme, A. and Howe, C. (1993). Gender and dialogue in secondary school physics. *Gender and education*, 5, 2, 93, 191–209.

Toohey, K. (1992). We teach English as a second language to bilingual students. In: B. Burnaby and A. Cummings (Eds.), *Socio-political aspects of ESL*. (pp. 87–96). Toronto: OISE.

Toohey, K. (1996a). *Learning ESL in a Punjabi Sikh school: A community of practice perspective*. Research proposal-Centre of Excellence for Research on Immigration and Integration. Simon Fraser University. Burnaby, B.C., Canada.

Toohey, K. (1996b). Learning English as a second language in kindergarten: A community of practice perspective. *The Canadian Modern Language Review*, 52 (4), 549–576.

Toohey, K. (1997). 'Breaking them up. Taking them away': ESL students in grade one. *TESOL Quarterly*, 32, 61–84.

Toohey, K. (2000). *Learning English at school: Identity, social relations and classroom practice*. Clevedon, UK: Multilingual Matters Ltd.

Toohey, K., Waterstone, B. and Julé-Lemke, A. (2000). Community of learners, carnival and participation in a Punjabi Sikh classroom. *The Canadian Modern Language Review*, 56, 423–438.

Troemel-Ploetz, S. (1991). Selling the apolitical. *Discourse and Society*, 2.4. pp. 489–502.

Trudeau, P. E. (1984). Statement by the Prime Minister in the House of Commons, October 8, 1971. In: J. Mallea and J. Young (Eds.), *Cultural diversity and Canadian education*. Ottawa: Carleton University Press.

Trudgill, P. (1974). *Sociolinguistics: An introduction.* Middlesex: Penguin.

Turner, L. H. and Sterk, H. M. (Eds.) (1994). *Differences that make a difference: Examining the assumptions in gender research.* London: Bergin and Garvey.

Tutchell, E. (1990). Contradictory identities: Theory into practice. In: E. Tutchell (Ed.), *Dolls and dungarees: Gender issues in the primary school curriculum.* (pp. 7–13). Milton Keyes: Open University Press.

Vancouver Sun. (1999). www.vancouversun.com. Keyword: Punjabi.

Vandrick, S. (1999a). Who's afraid of critical and feminist pedagogies? *TESOL Matters,* February/March, 9 (1).

Vandrick, S. (1999b). The case for more research on female students in the ESL/EFL classroom. *TESOL Matters,* 9 (2) April/May, 16.

Vygotsky, L. S. (1981). The genesis of higher mental functions. In: J. V. Wertsch (Ed.), *The concept of activity in soviet psychology.* Armonk, NY: M. E. Sharpe.

Walker, R. and Adelman, C. (1975). *A guide to classroom observation.* London: Routledge.

Walkerdine, V. (1990). *Schoolgirl fictions.* London: Versco.

Walkerdine, V. (1997). *Daddy's girl: Young girls and popular culture.* London: Macmillan Press.

Walkerdine, V. and Lucey, H. (1989). *Democracy in the kitchen: Regulating mothers and socializing daughters.* London: Virago Press.

Wareing, S. (1994). Gender differences in language use. In: J. Sunderland (Ed.), *Exploring gender: Questions and implications for English language education.* (pp. 34–38). New York: Prentice Hall.

Wareing, S. and Thomas, L. (Eds.) (1999). *Language, society and power.* London: Routledge.

Weiner, G. (1985). Equal opportunities, feminism and girls' education: Introduction. In: G. Weiner (Ed.), *Just a bunch of girls: Feminist approaches to schooling.* (pp. 1–13). Milton Keyes: Open University Press.

Weir, C. J. and Roberts, J. R. (1994). *Evaluation in ELT.* Oxford: Blackwell.

Wells, M. (1996). From margin to center: Interventions supporting gender equity in the Toronto Board of Education. *Women's Studies International Forum,* 19 (4), 371–380.

Wertsch, J. V. (1991). *Voices of the mind.* Cambridge, Mass.: Harvard University Press.

West, C. and Zimmerman, D. (1983). Small insults: A study of interruptions in cross-sex conversations between unacquainted persons. In: B. Thorne, C. Kramarae, C. N. Henley (Eds.), *Language, gender and society.* Rowley: Newbury House.

West, C. and Zimmerman, D. H. (1987). Doing gender. *Gender and society,* 1, 125–151.

Whorf, B. J. (1956). *Language, thought and reality.* Cambridge, Mass.: MIT Press.

Whyte, J., Deem, R., Kant, L. and Cruickshank, M. (Eds.) (1985). *Girl friendly schooling.* London: Methuen.

Wilden, A. (1981). *Jacques Lacan: The language of the self.* Translation, notes, and commentary. Baltimore: Johns Hopkins University Press.

Willett, J. (1996). Research as gendered practice. *TESOL Quarterly,* 30 (2), 344–347.

Windass, A. (1989). Classroom practices and organization. In: C. Skelton (Ed.), *Whatever happens to little women: Gender and primary schooling.* (pp. 38–49). Milton Keyes, UK: Open University Press.

Wodak, R. (1996). *Disorders of discourse.* London: Longman.

Wodak, R. (Ed.) (1997). *Gender and discourse.* London: Sage.

Wolpe, A. (1988). *Within school walls: The role of discipline, sexuality and the curriculum.* London: Routledge.

Wollstonecraft, M. (1791/1989). *A vindication of the rights of women.* London: Prometheus.

Women of South Asian Descent Collective (Ed.) (1993). *Our feet walk the sky.* San Francisco: Aunt Lute Books.

Woodward, C. V. (1986). Between Little Rock and a hard place. *New Republic* (February), 29–33.

Yates, L. (1997). Gender, equity and the boys debate: What sort of challenge is it? *British Journal of Sociology of Education,* 18 (3), 337–347.

Yepez, M. (1994). An observation of gender-specific teacher behavior in the ESL classroom. *Sex Roles,* 30, 121–133.

Younger, M., Warrington, M. and Williams, J. (1999). The gender gap and classroom interactions: Reality and rhetoric. *British Journal of Sociology in Education,* 20 (3), 325–341.

Zimmerman, D. and West, C. (1975). Sex roles, interruptions and silences in conversation. In: B. Thorne and N. Henley (Eds.), *Language and sex: Difference and dominance.* (pp. 105–129). Massachusetts: Newbury House.

Index